A Guide to the Records of

Minnesota's Public Lands

by Gregory Kinney and Lydia Lucas

Minnesota Historical Society

Division of Archives and Manuscripts

1985

International Standard Book Number 0-87351-192-1
Library of Congress Catalog Card Number 85-62761

Printed with funds provided by a grant from the Legislative Commission on Minnesota Resources.

TABLE OF CONTENTS

Introduction	1
State Land Office	
History	5
Records	8
State Auditor	
Land Department Records	25
Other Records	33
Conservation Department	
Lands and Minerals Division Records	34
Other Records	36
Natural Resources Department Records	38
Governor's Office Records	40
Secretary of State Records	42
Other Land-Related Records of State Agencies	43
U.S. Surveyor General of Minnesota	
History	47
Records	50
U.S. General Land Office	
History	58
General Records	64
Map Showing Land Offices and their Opening Dates	66
Land District Histories	67
District Land Office Records	85
Northern Pacific Railway Company Land Department Records	114
Laws Relating to Minnesota Lands	117
Bibliography	121

INTRODUCTION

The records described in this guide document the state of Minnesota's acquisition, sale, and management of its trust fund, railroad grant, and related lands, as well as the federal land survey of Minnesota and the initial transfer of title to public lands from the federal government to the state or to private parties. The approximately 800 cubic feet of records were created primarily by four agencies: the State Land Office, the Land Department of the State Auditor's office, the U.S. General Land Office in Minnesota, and the U.S. Surveyor General for Minnesota. The guide also summarizes land-related records in other state agencies, with individual descriptions of particularly pertinent records series.

Under the Enabling Act of February 26, 1857, by which Minnesota became a state, as well as under other laws relating to public land states in general, the federal government granted Minnesota certain **trust fund lands.** The sale or lease of these lands was intended to generate funds for support of the common (public) school system, for a state university and an agricultural college, for the erection of public buildings, and for internal improvements such as road construction. Ultimately, most of the income from the various trust fund lands was devoted to schools and other educational purposes.

Swamp lands and school lands comprised the two largest categories of these granted lands. **Swamp lands**--marshes or floodplains that were considered unfit for cultivation--were granted to the state under an act of 1860 to encourage their reclamation and disposal. Minnesota received a total of more than 4,700,000 acres of such lands (state and federal figures differ, and there was considerable controversy over what constituted "swamp land" as defined by the grant). However, the state made an annual appropriation for land drainage, and proceeds from the sale or lease of swamp lands were used for state institutions and common schools. The **school lands** granted to the state under the Enabling Act consisted of sections 16 and 36 in every township, or alternative (indemnity) selections if portions of these sections were already disposed of or contained bodies of water. Over 2,900,000 acres of land (state and federal figures differ here, also) accrued to the state under this grant.

The Enabling Act also granted Minnesota ten sections (6400 acres) of land for the purpose of erecting or completing **public buildings** at the seat of government; 72 sections (46,080 acres) to support a **state university** (in addition to another 72 sections reserved in 1851 for a "territorial university"); and up to 72 sections of land adjoining **salt springs**, the majority of which the legislature also designated for the use of the state university. The Morrill Act of July 2, 1862, entitled Minnesota to another 120,000 acres in support of an **agricultural college**, which became a component of the state university as well. (A provision of the Morrill Act that counted double those selected lands that lay within the limits of a railroad grant resulted in the actual transfer of 94,439 acres.) The state's entitlement to 500,000 acres of **internal**

improvement land under a federal act of September 4, 1841, was affirmed in 1866. A state law of 1865 appropriated 525,000 acres of state swamp lands for the benefit of **state institutions**: an insane asylum, deaf and dumb institute, state prison, and three normal schools.

The state-owned lands described in this guide consist almost entirely of these categories of trust fund lands. Interspersed in larger series are a few records pertaining to **Volstead lands** (parcels acquired in 1963 under the 1908 Volstead Act, which permitted liens against unpaid drainage assessments) and to a few miscellaneous land transfers.

Except for the school lands, trust fund lands were transferred on the basis of selection lists prepared by the state and submitted to the U.S. General Land Office for approval. The process of selection, submission, and approval for these lands spanned several decades, from 1858 until well into the twentieth century.

Once granted or patented to the state, the lands could be resold to the public, with the buyer receiving a final patent (deed) to the land after all principal and accrued interest had been paid. Sales of trust fund lands were held once or perhaps twice a year in each county within which lands were available. Lists of land being offered for sale were published and circulated prior to the sale. Most lands were purchased on long-term contracts, usually 40 years, although numerous parcels were paid for in full long before that length of time had passed. It was not uncommon for a tract of land to change hands several times between the initial purchase and the issuance of a patent.

In addition to the trust fund lands, various acts of Congress between the years 1857 and 1866 granted land concessions to Minnesota to aid in the construction of certain railroads. As each portion of a qualifying rail line was completed, the railroad company received title to a designated amount of public land, usually the odd-numbered sections within a specified distance each side of the line, or to indemnity selections for any of this land that was deficient in area or already claimed. These lands were transferred from the federal government to the state of Minnesota, which in turn deeded them to the railroads, who then sold them to recover construction costs.

The railroads affected by these laws were the St. Paul and Pacific, St. Paul and Sioux City, Minnesota Central, Winona and St. Peter, Southern Minnesota, Lake Superior and Mississippi, and Hastings and Dakota and their predecessor and successor companies. The Northern Pacific Railway Company received a grant of land directly from Congress. The state of Minnesota also regranted portions of its swamp lands, totaling about 2,900,000 acres, to some of these and other railroad companies: Lake Superior and Mississippi, Southern Minnesota, Minnesota Central, Taylors Falls and Lake Superior, St. Paul and Chicago, Minneapolis and St. Cloud, Duluth and Iron Range, and Little Falls and Dakota.

The state has also acquired other tracts of land, for such purposes as state parks and forests, game refuges, wildlife management areas, conservation reserves, and wetlands. Files pertaining to these lands are scattered among the records of the Conservation and Natural Resources departments. There are voluminous files on the management of timber, minerals, and other resources on state lands. Occasional records pertain to boundaries, timber, ownership rights, and other matters relating to Indian reservations in the state. None of these records are described in detail in this guide, although summary guide entries note the primary aggregations of such data. In addition, information on lands forfeited to the state for non-payment of taxes are found with the records of many individual counties, as well as scattered among a number of state agency files.

The area comprising present-day Minnesota was originally part of the federal public domain. Those lands that were not granted to the state or to railroads or reserved to Indian ownership were subject to acquisition by private parties directly from the federal government. The U.S. General Land Office, created in 1812, was responsible for managing the disposition of the federal domain. The records of its Minnesota land offices, beginning with the first lands opened for entry (purchase) in 1848, document both the initial transfer of title to all lands in the state and the administration of the land entry, payment, title, grant, and contest system for the federal lands.

Before any land could be officially opened for sale or transfer, it had to be surveyed. The office of the U.S. Surveyor General of Minnesota was responsible for conducting the original government survey of the public domain in the state. Its records span the period from 1848, when the earliest land surveys were conducted in southeastern Minnesota, to 1907, when the survey of Minnesota was essentially complete, and consist of both the survey notes and plats and a variety of administrative records.

All of the records described in this guide are housed in the Minnesota State Archives at the Minnesota Historical Society, Division of Archives and Manuscripts. Current administrative records for lands still owned by the state, which continue or supplant some of the series listed herein, remain with the Land Bureau of the Minnesota Department of Natural Resources (DNR). Increments are transferred to the State Archives from time to time. Several series of State Land Office records, as well as the original entry tract books of the U.S. General Land Office, have been microfilmed and the originals withdrawn from general use. The microfilm copies are described in this guide. The originals are either in the State Archives or scheduled for transfer from the DNR. Some series of administrative records may in the future be microfilmed in lieu of permanent retention of the originals.

The series descriptions in this guide are supplemented by individual box content, folder title, and/or volume lists, as well as occasional detailed narratives or item lists, all of which are available in the reading room of the Division of Archives and Manuscripts. Photocopies of these finding aids may be purchased as well. An assortment of published documents relating to state lands and land sales, minerals, timber, and state parks, issued primarily by the Conservation Department and the State Auditor, are also available in the State Archives or at the Minnesota Historical Society Reference Library. The State Planning Agency maintains a wide range of current land status and land use data on Minnesota in general and state-owned lands in particular.

A number of individuals and agencies contributed directly or indirectly to the production of this guide. Processing, inventorying, and description of most of the State Land Office, U.S. General Land Office, and U.S. Surveyor General records, as well as microfilming of the vital land transfer and ownership records, were supported by an appropriation of funds from the Legislative Commission on Minnesota Resources (LCMR), which also funded the publication of this guide. Commission members Robert E. Hansen, executive director, and John R. Velin, administrative assistant, were particularly enthusiastic supporters of this project, as was Donald P. Yaeger, project manager for the state's Land Management Information Center. Project archivist Gregory Kinney carried out most of the LCMR-funded processing and microfilming work, assisted at various stages by Cathy Emkovik and Geraldine Nielsen and by members of the Division of Archives and Manuscripts permanent staff.

Rodney W. Rowe of the DNR Land Bureau offered valuable advice and assistance in identifying and assessing the vital records of the State Land Office and in transferring them to the State Archives for microfilming and storage, and the DNR's Rodney W. Sando provided the necessary administrative support. Roderick H. Squires, associate professor of geography at the University of Minnesota, supplied the sketch maps that illustrate the U.S. General Land Office administrative histories, critiqued the text of the GLO section, and in general contributed the perspective of a longtime user of these records.

STATE LAND OFFICE

The State Land Office was established in 1862, to "have the general charge and supervision of all lands belonging to the State" (General Laws 1862 c62 s3). It received, managed, and sold trust fund lands granted to the state of Minnesota by various acts of the U.S. Congress; served as a conduit for the federal lands granted to various railroads to aid in the construction of their lines in the state; held and resold lands forfeited to the state for non-payment of taxes; and was involved in the acquisition and management of assorted other lands acquired by the state.

Minnesota began making provision for the management and sale of its trust fund lands almost immediately upon attaining statehood. The state constitution, ratified on October 13, 1857, authorized the disposal at public sale of the school lands and required that the proceeds remain a perpetual school fund. Laws passed in 1858 and 1861 established penalties for trespass (specifically, cutting timber and hay) on lands granted to the state by Congress for schools, universities, or internal improvements (Laws 1858 c17 and Laws 1861 c12). Two laws passed in March of 1861 established state boards of commissioners of school lands and of public lands, both consisting of the governor, the attorney general, and the superintendent of public instruction. One was to oversee the school lands and supervise their sale, and the other to supervise the survey and management of all classes of state lands (Laws 1861 c14 and c13).

No land sales were held under the aegis of either of these commissions. The 1862 law abolished both of them and replaced them with the State Land Office, making the state auditor the *ex officio* land commissioner and authorizing him to oversee, sell, lease, and dispose of all state lands.

The State Land Office was not a separate state agency. The state auditor, in his capacity as state land commissioner, was in charge of the trust fund and grant lands during the period of their most active acquisition and disposal, 1862-1931. The name "State Land Office" was used rather inconsistently on official documents relating to state lands during the 1860s, until the land administration function became well established. As the auditor's office grew in size and complexity, a Land Department was created to handle sales and transfers of trust fund lands, as well as to manage timber and mineral resources on unsold trust fund and other state-owned lands.

The auditor's duties and responsibilities for the administration of state lands were terminated in 1931. The functions and records of the Land Department were transferred to the Lands and Minerals Division and the Forestry Division of the newly organized Conservation Department (Laws 1931 c186), although logistical problems and a controversy over the constitutionality of this action delayed the effective transfer until 1933. In 1967 the Lands Section of the Lands and Minerals Division was merged with the Forestry Division to form the Lands and Forestry Division (Laws 1967 c905). This division was carried over as such when the Conservation Department became the Natural Resources Department (DNR) in 1971 (Laws 1969 c1129). In about 1973 state land administration was again made a separate function with the creation of the DNR's Land Bureau (DNR Biennial Report, 1972-1974).

The record series listed under State Land Office are those records of the selection, sale, and status of state trust fund and related lands that constitute the state's master record of these lands. The deed records, patent records, and approved lists are the original documents conveying title from the federal government to the state of Minnesota, and from the state to the initial private purchaser or grantee. Title searchers have found that the deeds and patents were not systematically recorded with the county registers of deeds, and thus the State Land Office records constitute a vital link in the chain of title to these Minnesota lands. Other State Land Office series are administrative records of sales, payments, and status of the lands. Most of the records were transferred from the auditor to the Conservation Department when responsibility for the lands was transferred. Nearly all of these series are now inactive.

Correspondence and administrative files regarding all aspects of the acquisition, transfer, management, and disposal of state lands and of their timber and mineral resources are listed under State Auditor: Land Department (pages 25-32) and in various subgroups and series of the Conservation and Natural Resources departments and the governor's office (pages 34-41). Files in other state agencies (pages 42-46) give additional insight into the administration of these lands. Records concerning the sale, transfer, and status of the remainder of the public domain in Minnesota are listed under U.S. General Land Office (pages 64-113).

List of Series:

Abstract of State Land, 1940-ca.1978. 10 vols.
[Abstract of Unpatented State Land], 1911-1915. 1 vol.
Abstracts of Sales, 1882-1981. 6 rolls microfilm.
Appraisals of State Land, 1862-ca.1968. 36.0 c.f.
Approved List: State Experimental Forest, 1905. 1 folder.
Approved Lists, 1858-1963. 1 roll microfilm.
Approved Lists: Congressional Railroad Land Grants, 1860-1931. 2 rolls microfilm.
Approved Lists: Congressional Railroad Land Grants (Supplement), 1894-1906. 3 folders.
Approved Lists: Swamp Lands, 1865-1912. 1 roll microfilm.
Approved Lists: Swamp Lands (Set 2), 1865-1959. 1.3 c.f.
Drainage Assessment (Ditch) Records, 1907-1931. 4 vols.
Duluth and Iron Range Railroad: Records of Swamp Land Selections, 1913-1917. 0.7 c.f.
[Maps: List], December 1892. 1 vol.

Maps: Miscellaneous, undated and 1858-1920. 1.0 c.f.
Maps: Northern Pacific Railroad Rights of Way Across State Lands, undated and 1892. 2 folders.
Maps: Railroad Maps, 1857-1911. 7.0 c.f.
Memorandum of Sale of State Land, 1903-1978. 12.0 c.f.
Miscellaneous Deeds, 1887-1943. 1 roll microfilm.
Miscellaneous Trust Fund Land Lists and Correspondence, 1857-1938. 0.9 c.f.
Patent Records, State Trust Fund Lands, 1863-1978. 31 rolls microfilm.
Railroad Deed Record, 1864-1942. 4 rolls microfilm.
Railroad Land Grant Patents: United States to Minnesota, 1875-1935. 1 roll microfilm.
Railroad Swamp Land Selection Lists, 1880-1926. 2.6 c.f.
Record of Land Examinations on Chippewa Indian Reservations, 1904, 1908. 1 vol. and 2 folders.
Record of Leases on Public Building Lands, 1891-1895. 1 vol.
Record of Payments on State Land Contracts: Internal Improvement Lands, 1872-1943. 5 vols. and 3 partial vols.
Record of Payments on State Land Contracts: Reform School Lands, 1892-1913. 1 vol.
Record of Payments on State Land Contracts: School and Related Lands, 1862-1943. 69 vols.
Record of Payments on State Land Contracts: State Institution Lands, 1882-1915. 2 vols. and 1 partial vol.
Record of Payments on State Land Contracts: Swamp Lands, 1901-1943. 19 vols.
Record of Sales: State Trust Fund Lands, 1862-1879. 4 rolls microfilm.
Record of Sales: State Trust Fund Lands, ca.1878-ca.1940. 6 rolls microfilm.
Record of Sales: State Trust Fund Lands (Supplement), ca.1883-ca.1936. 7 vols.
School and Other State Land to be Offered for Sale: Published Lists, 1905-1914. 1 vol.
Special Certificate Record, 1870-1974. 1 roll microfilm.
State Subdivisions Plat Book, undated. 1 roll microfilm.
State Subdivisions Plat Files, undated and 1862-1909. 2 folders and 1 oversize folder.
State Trust Fund Land Certificates, 1862-1984. 79.0 c.f.
Swamp Land Miscellaneous Lists and Correspondence, undated and 1862-1923. 1.6 c.f.
Swamp Land Patents: United States to Minnesota, 1865-1960. 2 rolls microfilm.
Swamp Land Record, ca.1860-1931. 3 rolls microfilm.
Swamp Land Selection Lists, 1875-1915. 1.75 c.f.

STATE LAND OFFICE RECORDS

Abstract of State Land, 1940-ca.1978. 9.0 c.f. (10 vols.)

A cumulative administrative record of the status of each parcel of state trust fund land that was unsold or unpatented as of 1940. The abstract was initially compiled in 1940-1941 (abstracts for a few counties appear to date from 1936), and annotations record any subsequent changes in the status of a parcel. The abstract records both original sales and resales of relinquished, tax-forfeited, and payment-delinquent land.

The abstract is arranged by county, thereunder by type of trust fund, and thereunder by range, township, section, and fractional section. Unsold parcels are simply listed in the appropriate place with no annotations. For parcels that had been sold but not patented prior to 1940, the abstract may include the following information as appropriate: certificate number, date of sale, date final payment was received or patent issued, unpaid balance, the last year an interest payment was received (for delinquent land), tax status of the parcel, date the parcel was reoffered for sale, date of the most recent appraisal, notations if the parcel includes lakeshore or is in a state forest, and occasional explanatory remarks.

There are no abstracts for several counties. Apparently there were no unpatented trust fund lands in these counties as of 1940.

A new set of abstracts was compiled in about 1978 and is still (1985) in use by the Department of Natural Resources Land Bureau. Parcels patented between 1940 and 1978 were eliminated from the new abstracts.

Arrangement: By county in approximate alphabetical order.

Related Records: The Abstract of State Land appears to be a successor to the **Record of Sales** (pages 20-21).

[Abstract of Unpatented State Land], 1911-1915. 1 vol.

Lists, by county, of parcels of trust fund lands sold prior to 1875 but not yet paid up and patented. Compiled, probably in 1911, to identify those parcels for which the forty-year payment limit on the initial land certificates was about to expire, as evidenced by accompanying copies of form letters from the state auditor to county treasurers. Each entry gives legal description, certificate number, purchaser's name, and amount of principal unpaid; for most parcels, a date (1911-1915) on which the principal was paid has been added.

Abstracts of Sales, 1882-1981. 6 rolls microfilm (16 vols.: 8.5 c.f.)

Abstracts of sales of the various categories of trust fund lands by the state of Minnesota to private parties. Sales were conducted at the county level through public auction by the county auditor or treasurer. Some time after each sale, a report on the lands sold was sent to the State Land Office, where the information was recorded as abstracts of sales. The abstracts were recorded by date of sale and thereunder by county, in the order in which the land office received the reports from the county officials. Because of delays in reporting, sales may not appear in strict chronological order. The abstracts for each sale are arranged by range, town, section, and fractional section. Each fractional section has a certificate number that was consecutively assigned as the abstract was recorded.

The abstracts list, for each parcel of land sold, the certificate number, legal description, appraised value per acre, total acreage, price per acre, total amount to be paid, down payment, unpaid balance, first year's interest on the balance, purchaser's name, and record of any forfeited sales. No subsequent payment or patent data are included. Some volumes contain indexes, not always complete, that cite the page(s) on which the abstracts for each county are found. Abstracts are present for the following categories of lands: school lands, 1882-1981; internal improvement lands, 1882-1969; state institution lands, 1890-1907; swamp lands, 1902-1981; agricultural college lands, 1882-1909; public buildings lands, 1901-1939; university lands, 1882-1964; rural credit lands, 1947; and Volstead lands, 1963-1971.

Appraisals of State Land, 1862-ca.1968. 36.0 c.f. (13 oversize and 11 double oversize boxes)

A record of appraisals made on state trust fund land prior to its being offered for sale. The appraisals were made to establish the minimum price for which a tract would be sold. The series includes appraisals for original sales and for resales of payment-delinquent and tax-forfeited land. The appraisals fall into three chronological sequences: 1862-1921, 1921-ca.1947, and ca.1933-ca.1968.

Each appraisal sheet (one section or portion of a section is recorded on a sheet) gives the range, town, and section of the tract appraised; date of appraisal; and type of trust fund the tract belonged to. General information given for each section includes distances to nearest village and post office, predominate nationality of area residents, condition of roads on or near the appraised parcels, extent of naturally reproducing timber on the parcels, and general comments on the quality of the land and its potential uses. The sheet also provides detailed descriptions of each quarter-quarter section appraised. These list the value and type of timber on the quarter section; soil type; acres of meadow, swamp, uplands, and waste; acres of cleared land; descriptions of any improvements on the land; appraised value per acre; and uses to which the land may be adapted.

Appraisals made after 1921 include a coded plat drawing of the section indicating the parcels covered by the appraisal and sketching or noting data on the terrain and vegetation. After 1933 resale appraisals usually indicate the last year in which the interest had been paid on delinquent land and the last year taxes had been paid on tax-forfeited land. There is also usually a notation of the year when the parcel was formally declared delinquent or forfeit.

The series also includes one box of appraisals made for the Land Exchange Commission during 1942-1948. These appraisals were made for trust fund land in Carlton, Cass, Cook, Itasca, Koochiching, Lake, Lake of the Woods, and St. Louis counties that were part of national forests, state forests, or other reserves and were to be exchanged for other federal land.

Arrangement: By county and thereunder by range, township, and section within three chronological sequences.

Approved List: State Experimental Forest, 1905. 1 folder
A list and plats of lands approved for patenting to Minnesota for use as a state experimental forest as provided by a congressional act of April 28, 1904 (33 Stat. 536).

The act of 1904 allowed the state to select 20,000 acres from the federal domain to be used as an experimental forest. The approved list certifies that the selected tracts were not subject to any other claim or reservation. The list gives the legal description of the approved tracts and the plats illustrate their location in townships 63 and 64, range 13, St. Louis County (the present Burntside State Forest).

Approved Lists, 1858-1963. 1 roll microfilm (8 vols.: 2.5 c.f.)
Approved lists for various categories of state trust fund lands, selected by the state of Minnesota from the federal domain for specified public purposes under a number of congressional grants. The approved lists were issued through the local and district offices of the U.S. General Land Office and certify that the lands selected by the state were not subject to any prior claim or reservation. Approved lists are present for the following categories of land: indemnity school lands, 1858-1960; agricultural college lands, 1867-1879; internal improvement lands, 1867-1874, 1906-1907; salt spring lands, 1871-1916; public building lands, 1863; university lands, 1854-1915; and Volstead lands, 1963.

Each approved list gives list number, land district through which the selections were made, date of selection, legal descriptions and acreages of the parcels selected, and dates the selections were approved by the commissioner of the General Land Office and the secretary of the interior.

Finding Aids: Indexes by range and township accompany the approved lists.

Approved Lists: Congressional Railroad Land Grants, 1860-1931. 2 rolls microfilm (9 vols.: 3.0 c.f.)
Lists of lands approved by the U.S. General Land Office for transfer to those railroad companies that had received grants of land from Congress to aid in construction of their lines. Under the terms of its grant, a company was entitled to a specified amount of public land for each mile of track constructed, usually the odd-numbered sections within six miles each side of the track, reserved to the railroad after the route of its line had been set. If any of this land was deficient in area or subject to prior claim or reservation, the railroad was entitled to select an equivalent amount of public land within wider limits as indemnity. The railroad company filed selection lists with the local federal land office for these indemnity lands. The approved lists certified that the indemnity lands were not subject to any prior claim or reservation.

The approved lists were issued for the Southern Minnesota Railroad; Winona and St. Peter Railroad; St. Paul and Sioux City Railroad; Minnesota Central Railway; Hastings and Dakota Railroad; Minnesota Valley Railroad; St. Paul and Pacific Railroad; Lake Superior and Mississippi Railroad; Northern Pacific Railway; and their predecessors and successors. Each list gives railroad name, land office through which selections were made, citation to the original grant, legal descriptions and acreages of the parcels approved, total acreage approved by the list, and dates the selections were approved by the commissioner of the General Land Office and the secretary of the interior.

Arrangement: By railroad.

Finding Aids: Each volume is prefaced by a location index; there is also a consolidated location index.

Approved Lists: Congressional Railroad Land Grants (Supplement), 1894-1906. 0.1 c.f. (3 folders)

Additional approved lists for the Northern Pacific Railway, the St. Paul and Pacific Railroad and its successors, and the St. Paul, Minneapolis and Manitoba Railway that are missing from the microfilmed set.

Approved Lists: Swamp Lands, 1865-1912. 1 roll microfilm (1.0 c.f.)

An incomplete set of lists of swamp lands submitted to the U.S. General Land Office and certified by that office as qualifying for transfer to the state of Minnesota.

The swamp land grant, authorized by congressional acts of September 28, 1850, and March 12, 1860, entitled the state of Minnesota to select from the public domain all "swamp and overflowed lands" unsuitable for cultivation and to dispose of the land for such public purposes as the legislature saw fit. The swamp land approved lists, as issued by the General Land Office, certified that the tracts selected by the state qualified under the grant's definition of swamp and overflowed lands and were not subject to any adverse claim. The approved lists did not transfer title, but were a preliminary step to the issuance of a patent.

The lists are arranged by land district and thereunder by date of approval by the secretary of the interior. They include the following information: list number; land district through which the selections were made; description of the tracts selected, citing range, town, section, and fractional section; acreage of the tract; total acreage approved in the list; and date approved by the commissioner of the General Land Office and the secretary of the interior.

The swamp land approved lists were originally dispersed among the records of the U.S. General Land Office and the Minnesota auditor's office in the State Archives, and have been brought together in a single file.

Related Records: **Swamp Land Patents: United States to Minnesota** (page 23); **Swamp Land Selection Lists** (page 24).

Approved Lists: Swamp Lands (Set 2), 1865-1959. 1.3 c.f. (7 vols. and 5 folders)

Lists of swamp lands submitted to the U.S. General Land Office and certified by that office as qualifying for transfer to the state of Minnesota.

The lists are arranged, for the most part, by land district and thereunder by date of approval by the secretary of the interior. List numbers were originally assigned in separate sequences for each land district. After about 1895 list numbers were assigned in a single sequence encompassing all land districts.

This set of swamp land approved lists was originally in the custody of the Department of Natural Resources, Land Bureau, and is more complete than the microfilmed series.

Finding Aids: Volumes and/or lists include tract indexes.

Drainage Assessment (Ditch) Records, 1907-1931. 1.0 c.f. (4 vols.)
A record of the parcels of state land against which assessments were levied for the construction of various county and judicial ditches. Each tract of land that would be benefitted by the construction of these drainage ditches was assessed. The state of Minnesota paid the assessments on state lands that had not yet been sold.

Under each county and ditch number is itemized, for each quarter-quarter section, the amount of assessment and interest. Summary payment data are also noted.

Finding Aids: A location index appears at the beginning of each volume.

Duluth and Iron Range Railroad: Records of Swamp Land Selections, 1913-1917. 0.7 c.f. (1 folder and 1 bundle)
An itemized record, by parcel, of swamp lands deeded to the Duluth and Iron Range Railroad under Minnesota Special Laws of 1875, Chapter 54; and correspondence and lists, 1913-1917, regarding the completion of this land grant.

The 1875 law and its successors (Special Laws 1876 c241 and Special Laws 1883 c69) entitled the Duluth and Iron Range Railroad to ten sections of swamp land for each mile of completed road, to be selected within ten miles either side of the line or from other swamp lands in St. Louis, Lake, and Cook counties to make up any deficiencies. Notes in the file comparing granted lands with the State Land Office's "Swamp Land Record" indicate that the total acreage was to have been 606,720 acres.

In 1914 the railroad pressed claims to lands it felt entitled to receive as indemnity for lands lost to it through previous deed and title problems, occupation by other railroads' rights of way, overlapping land descriptions, and surveying errors, totalling 5966.87 acres. The state allowed an entitlement of 5448.52 acres.

The bulk of this file consists of sheets (620 pages) that appear to itemize the status of each parcel of land surveyed for possible grant to the Duluth and Iron Range Railroad. They record each parcel's legal description, evidence of title, whether deeded to and/or filed on by the Duluth and Iron Range Railroad or for state institutions, whether vacant, and whether the state's claim was rejected. They are accompanied by various summary sheets, as well as the folder of correspondence and lists.

Related Records: **Railroad Swamp Land Selection Lists** (page 16).

[Maps: List], December 1892. 1 vol.
Entitled "Index to Maps on File in the State Land Office," this five-page volume lists railroad location and construction maps, maps of military roads, and miscellaneous maps filed with the State Land Office

between about 1862 and 1892. Many, but not all, of these are among the State Land Office maps described below; the State Land Office map files also contain maps not present on this list.

Maps: Miscellaneous, undated and 1858-1920. 1.0 c.f. (1 double oversize box)
Miscellaneous maps filed with or collected by the State Land Office, including town and city plats, roads, waterways, state lands, and Indian reservations.

They were identified on their original storage cartons as State Land Office maps, but most have no filing notation or other internal provenance data.

Maps: Northern Pacific Railroad Rights of Way Across State Lands, undated and 1892. 0.25 c.f. (2 folders)
Blueprint maps showing the line of the Northern Pacific across various sections of state swamp lands and internal improvement lands, submitted to the State Land Office in order to gain title to the rights of way in accordance with acts of Congress (July 2, 1864) and of the Minnesota legislature (Nov. 19, 1881).

Maps: Railroad Maps, 1857-1911. 7.0 c.f. (4 double oversize boxes and 4 map tubes)
Maps of railroad lines, submitted to the State Land Office in accordance with various acts of Congress or the Minnesota legislature that granted public lands and/or rights of way to the railroads to help support their construction. They are of three general types: location maps, which record the prospective route as surveyed and laid out; construction maps, showing the line as actually constructed, equipped, and put into operation; and right of way maps, showing portions of the line that crossed state land, usually with the dimensions and/or acreages of land claimed by the railroad for its right of way.

Although all of the maps had been identified upon receipt into the archives as being State Land Office maps, some are annotated as having been filed with the governor or secretary of state, and some contain no filing notation or other internal provenance data.

Arrangement: All maps for a given railroad are listed together; railroads are listed in partial alphabetical order.

Memorandum of Sale of State Land, 1903-1978. 12.0 c.f. (51 vols.)
Lists of state trust fund land to be offered for sale in a given year. The lists were prepared by the State Land Office and sent to the county auditors who were to conduct the sales. They list each parcel of land offered for sale and include both original sales and resales of forfeited or delinquent lands. If a parcel was not sold the first time it was offered, it may be listed in more than one year. These volumes constitute an administrative record of sales, not legal instruments conveying title.

Information recorded: printed sheets, with columns filled in for county, sale date, township name, legal description of offered tracts, acreage, appraised value per acre, appraised value of timber and improvements, sale price per acre, purchaser's name and address, and remarks (type of trust fund). Later volumes contain more information categories than earlier volumes.

Arrangement: By year, thereunder alphabetically by county, thereunder by legal description of offered tracts.

Related Records: **Record of Sales: State Trust Fund Lands** (ca.1878-ca.1940, page 20) records similar (probably duplicate) information, but arranged primarily by county rather than year. **Abstracts of Sales** (page 8) summarize the actual sales, by date.

Miscellaneous Deeds, 1887-1943. 1 roll microfilm (2 vols.: 1.0 c.f.)
Primarily right of way, relinquishment, and quitclaim deeds affecting railroad lands. The right of way deeds were issued by the state of Minnesota for strips of state land through which a railroad line passed; they give date executed, grantor, grantee, legislative authorization for the right of way grant, purchase price, legal description of the fractional section(s) involved, and total acreage. The relinquishment deeds were issued by the state to the federal government for railroad grant lands that had been preempted by settlement; the settler then received title. They give citations to pertinent laws, claimant's name, legal description, acreage, and date of deed.

Quitclaim deeds conveyed a railroad corporation's interest in a parcel of its land grant back to the state of Minnesota. They give date of deed, grantee, grantor, price and/or other consideration paid, legal description, and sometimes the reason for reversion to the state. The volumes also include several other miscellaneous instruments of conveyance, including state land patents, judgments in condemnation proceedings, escheated estates, and final decrees in probate, all relating to railroad lands. Some deeds are accompanied by plat drawings or other documentation.

Finding Aids: Each volume contains two indexes, one organized by range and township and citing page number(s), the other organized by date of deed and citing grantee, grantor, type of deed, legal description, and page number. There is also a comprehensive index/abstract, arranged by survey location, to the right of way deeds recorded in these volumes and in the Railroad Deed Record.

Related Records: **Railroad Deed Record** (page 15) includes relinquishments and right of way deeds prior to 1887.

Miscellaneous Trust Fund Land Lists and Correspondence, 1857-1938. 0.9 c.f. (1 box)
Miscellaneous lists and correspondence relating to the selection, patenting, and sale of various types of state trust fund land. The series includes records relating to school, public building, state institution, university, and salt spring land.

Patent Records, State Trust Fund Lands, 1863-1978. 31 rolls microfilm (71 vols.: 34.5 c.f.)
The State Land Office's copies of the patents that constituted the original conveyance of title from the state of Minnesota to the purchasers of various categories of state trust fund lands. The printed forms are filled in with patent number; certificate number, which refers to the purchaser's initial filing for the parcel; name(s) of

patentee and any assignees; date of full payment on the land; legal description of the property citing section number and subdivision, township, range, and county, and usually giving the total acreage; and date the patent was executed.

The original of each patent was given to the purchaser of the land, who was responsible for registering it with the county recorder of deeds. Since this was not systematically done, especially in early years, this series constitutes the only complete record of original conveyance of the state's trust fund lands.

List of Subseries:

- School Lands, 1863-1942. 19 rolls (38 vols.)
  - Patent nos. 1-22,075. Includes indemnity school lands, interfiled prior to 1895 and thereafter in a separate sequence.
- School Lands Transferred, 1891-1942. 4 rolls (7 vols.)
  - Patent nos. 1-4131. Transferred from internal improvement lands (Laws 1891 c31).
- University Lands, 1880-1942. Partial roll (1 vol.)
  - Patent nos. 1-463.
- University Lands Transferred, 1897-1942. Partial roll (1 vol.)
  - Patent nos. 1-221. Transferred from internal improvement lands (Laws 1891 c31).
- Agricultural College Lands, 1872-1942. 1 roll (2 vols., 1 partial vol.)
  - Patent nos. 1-1248.
- Internal Improvement Lands, 1878-1942. 1 roll (2 vols.)
  - Patent nos. 1-1004.
- State Institution Lands, 1897-1942. Partial roll (1 vol., 1 partial vol.)
  - Patent nos. 1-693.
- Public Building Lands, 1902-1942. Partial roll (1 vol.)
  - Patent nos. 1-64.
- Reform School Lands, 1891-1902. Partial roll (1 vol.)
  - Patent nos. 1-11. D. W. Ingersoll's Addition to St. Paul.
- Swamp Lands, 1902-1942. 1 roll (2 vols.)
  - Patent nos. 1-1151.
- All Trust Fund Lands, 1942-1978. 3 rolls (14 vols.)
  - Patent nos. 33,001-39,700. Patents for all land categories, issued in a single sequence. Active series; patents are still being added.

Arrangement: By land category until 1942; thereunder by chronologically assigned patent number.

Railroad Deed Record, 1864-1942. 4 rolls microfilm (8 vols.: 4.0 c.f.) Handwritten copies of deeds issued by the state of Minnesota to private corporations for land grants authorized either by Congress or by the state legislature to aid in the construction of railroads. Upon completion of specified sections of line, the corporation was entitled to a deed to the land stipulated in the grant. The grants authorized by the state legislature were for designated swamp lands to which Minnesota had received title from the federal government.

Each deed gives the type and number of deed, railroad company to which the land was deeded, date, recapitulation of the original authorizing grant and its terms, citation to any legislation supplemental to the original grant, date the specified sections of the line were completed, governor's certification that terms of the grant were fulfilled, legal descriptions of lands conveyed, and total acreage deeded.

The records also include scattered railroad relinquishment and right of way deeds, as well as a few deeds and relinquishments for state roads, Indian reservations, salt spring lands, indemnity school lands, and the Cannon River Manufacturers Association. The relinquishment deeds were issued by the state to the federal government for railroad lands that had been settled prior to the authorization of the grant; the settler then received title to the land. They give legal description, acreage, and claimant's name. The right of way deeds were issued by the state to the railroad company for small strips of school land through which a railroad line passed. After about 1886, these are found in **Miscellaneous Deeds** (page 14).

Arrangement: Generally chronological.

Finding Aids: Each volume is prefaced by a location index and by a chronological list of deeds that cites grantee, acreage, and page number; there is also a consolidated location index.

Railroad Land Grant Patents: United States to Minnesota, 1875-1935. 1 roll microfilm (7 vols.: 3.0 c.f.)

The land grants represented by these patents were authorized by Congress to aid private corporations in the construction of designated railroads. Upon completion of specified sections of line, a railroad received title to the lands it had selected under the terms of its grant. These patents record the transfer of title to the selected lands from the federal government to the state of Minnesota, which in turn deeded them to the railroad company named in the patent. The patents in these seven volumes were issued for the St. Paul and Duluth Railroad; the St. Paul, Minneapolis and Manitoba Railway; its predecessor, the St. Paul and Pacific Railroad; the St. Paul and Northern Pacific Railway (formerly the Western Railroad Co.); and the Lake Superior and Mississippi Railroad.

The patents for each railroad summarize the provisions of the congressional authorization, including the proposed line's route and the conditions of the grant; date(s) the governor of Minnesota certified completion of the specified section(s); date(s) the selected lands were certified to Minnesota by the U.S. General Land Office; legal descriptions of the patented lands; total acreage patented within each township; aggregate acreage in the entire patent; and the date the patent was issued.

Arrangement: By railroad, thereunder by chronologically assigned patent number; after 1920 they are arranged by "list" number.

Finding Aids: Each volume is indexed, and there is also a general index.

Railroad Swamp Land Selection Lists, 1880-1926. 2.6 c.f. (3 boxes)

Lists of state swamp land selected by private companies as part of land grants from the state to aid in construction of railroads or for other purposes. The state legislature authorized the grants to these companies of designated swamp lands to which the state had previously acquired title from the federal government. The selection lists established the priority of the grantee company's claim to the selected lands.

The terms of the grants to the railroads varied somewhat, but most granted the company a specified amount of swamp land for each mile of line constructed. As the company completed a section of track, it submitted a selection list to the State Land Office describing the parcels it wished to acquire under its grant. The State Land Office examined the lists to determine if the selected parcels were subject to any prior claims or reservations. If no such claims existed the lands were deeded to the railroad. Lists are also present for lands selected by the Cannon River Manufacturers Association, which had received a grant for "developing and improving the water powers and manufacturing resources of the Cannon river" (Special Laws 1877 c244).

Each selection list gives the list number, name of grantee company, citations to the legislation authorizing the grant, date the selection list was filed, and legal descriptions of the parcels selected.

Filed with this series are several folders relating to congressional railroad grants. A summary of state legislation relating to railroad swamp land grants is filed in box 1.

Arrangement: By grantee company; thereunder by list number, followed by miscellaneous documents.

Related Records: **Railroad Deed Record** (page 15); **Swamp Land Record** (page 23); **Duluth and Iron Range Railroad: Records of Swamp Land Selections** (page 12).

Record of Land Examinations on Chippewa Indian Reservations, 1904, 1908. 1 vol. and 2 folders.

Land examination slips for swamp lands located on Minnesota's Chippewa Indian reservations. Two surveys are represented: one done in 1904 by Omar H. Case, appointed to represent the state of Minnesota during an examination conducted by W. B. Douglass of the U.S. General Land Office; and one done in 1908 by J. H. Beagle. They are accompanied by a list (undated) of the number of tracts in each township selected for Minnesota by the U.S. Surveyor General, examined, found to be swamp or dry, or not examined; and by a table (undated) showing, for each quarter-quarter section, the examination result (acres dry, acres swamp, and whether or not it was designated a swamp land tract).

Each examination slip covers an individual section of land within a township and contains a sketch map showing swamp areas and comments on vegetation and other pertinent data. Case's slips are pasted into a volume, indexed by range and township. His five-page report to state auditor S. G. Iverson, regarding the methodology of the U.S. survey and the current controversy over identification and designation of swamp lands, is pasted onto page 35; his examination slips were apparently prepared to provide evidence for the state of Minnesota's position that the majority of examined tracts were actually swamp lands.

Beagle's slips are foldered; cover sheets for each set of slips sent to the auditor are headed "State Land Examiner." Evidently representing a resurvey, they vary somewhat to considerably from Case's drawings and notes for the same tracts.

Record of Leases on Public Building Lands, 1891-1895. 1 vol.

A record of payments on leases for use of "public building" or "state capitol" trust fund land. An act of April 21, 1891 (Laws 1891 c132) authorized the state land commissioner to lease the land in Kandiyohi County that had been reserved to support construction of a state capitol and other public buildings.

The lease record gives the following information for each forty-acre parcel leased: lease number, date of lease, lessee, legal description of tract leased, rent per acre, and annual record of payments received.

Arrangement: By lease number.

Record of Payments on State Land Contracts: Internal Improvement Lands, 1872-1943. 3.5 c.f. (5 vols. and 3 partial vols.)

Record of annual payments made by purchasers of parcels of internal improvement land from the time the land was initially purchased until the final payment was made and a patent issued. A note in the front cover of volume A gives the total acreage as of January 28, 1880, as 499,686.51 acres.

Information recorded: legal description, number of acres (usually 40), price per acre, total purchase price, name of purchaser, date of purchase, certificate number, and payment schedule (columns for principal and interest paid each year). When payment on a parcel of land was completed, the volume records name of final patentee (who may or may not be the same as the initial purchaser), date of final payment, and patent number. Once a patent was issued, volumes for subsequent years note the purchaser and patent number (but no payment data) for parcels already patented, continuing the payment schedule for lands not yet patented.

A large proportion of the internal improvement lands are noted as having been transferred to the permanent school fund or the permanent university fund during the 1880s and 1890s.

Arrangement: By range and township within six chronological units, each covering a span of years for which a payment schedule was established.

Related Records: **Record of Payments . . .: School and Related Lands** (below), for land transferred from internal improvement lands.

Record of Payments on State Land Contracts: Reform School Lands, 1892-1913. 1 vol.

Record of annual payments made by purchasers of parcels of land in blocks 1-13 of Ingersoll's Addition to St. Paul, the former site of the state reform school. Following legislation to construct a permanent reform school near Red Wing in Goodhue County (Laws 1887 c200), the school's board of managers was directed to have its St. Paul site platted, appraised, and sold at auction by the commissioner of the

State Land Office, with proceeds credited to the reform school fund (General Laws 1889 c258).

Information recorded: certificate number, sale date, lot and block number, amount of sale, purchaser's name, amount of principal due, and payment schedule (annual interest payments 1892-1906, with a few later notations). The schedule notes that parts of blocks 3 and 4 were deeded to the city of St. Paul on June 1, 1909, under General Laws of 1909, Chapter 203; this law authorized their sale to the city for a public high school building and canceled all outstanding sale certificates. It also notes the sale of blocks 1, 2, 5, 6, 7, 9, and 10 to St. Paul on October 10, 1912, under General Laws of 1911, Chapter 163; this law directed their sale to the city for educational purposes and gives a synopsis of the ownership history of Ingersoll's Addition.

The volume is accompanied by a sample certificate of sale and a printed abstract of title to the lands comprising Ingersoll's Addition.

Arrangement: By block number.

Related Records: Plat of Ingersoll's Addition filed with **Maps: Miscellaneous** (page 13).

Record of Payments on State Land Contracts: School and Related Lands, 1862-1943. 58.0 c.f. (69 vols.)

Record of annual payments made by purchasers of parcels of school lands (sections 16 and 36 in each township). Also includes payment records for university, public building, salt spring, and agricultural college land; volumes for 1907-1943 were numbered by the State Land Office as part of the school lands series.

There are several volumes for each span of years for which a payment schedule was established. Each group of volumes is organized by meridian (4th or 5th) and range number, and thereunder by township number (one pair of facing pages per township), with a separate line for each quarter-quarter section of sections 16 and 36. Although the county name is noted on each page, the information is not organized by county.

Information recorded: Legal description, number of acres (usually 40, but occasionally aggregated or subdivided), price per acre, total purchase price, name of purchaser, date of purchase, certificate number, and payment schedule; name of final patentee, date of final payment, and patent number after payment was completed.

Parcels that were preempted, part of a military or Indian reserve or a state forest, in a lake or river, or otherwise unavailable are also noted.

Record of Payments on State Land Contracts: State Institution Lands, 1882-1915. 1.0 c.f. (2 vols. and 1 partial vol.)

Record of annual payments made by purchasers of parcels of land, the proceeds from the sale of which were dedicated to the support of state institutions.

Information recorded: Legal description, number of acres (usually 40), price per acre, total purchase price, name of purchaser, date of purchase, certificate number, and payment schedule; name of final patentee, date of final payment, and patent number after payment was completed. If an affidavit of improvement was filed, this is noted, with the affidavit number.

Record of Payments on State Land Contracts: Swamp Lands, 1901-1943. 17.0 c.f. (19 vols.)

Record of annual payments made by purchasers of parcels of swamp and overflow lands along the Mississippi River and its tributaries, the proceeds from which were dedicated to various educational and internal improvement purposes.

Each volume or group of volumes covers a span of years for which a payment schedule was established. Each volume is organized by range and township number (one pair of facing pages per township), with a separate line for each parcel (usually a quarter-quarter section).

Information recorded: Legal description, number of acres (generally 40, but with numerous variations), price per acre, total purchase price, name of purchaser, date of purchase, certificate number, and payment schedule; name of final patentee, date of final payment, and patent number after payment was completed. Entries for lands deeded to railroads are often recorded in red or purple ink in the early volumes. State forest and other reserved lands, tax-forfeited lands, and lands that reverted to the state are also noted. If an affidavit of improvement was filed, this is noted, with the affidavit number.

Related Records: Some of these swamp lands were transferred from **Record of Payments . . .: State Institution Lands**, vol. B (see Laws 1907 c385).

Record of Sales: State Trust Fund Lands, 1862-1879. 4 rolls microfilm (18 vols.: 4.5 c.f.)

Summary records of the sale of trust fund lands by the state of Minnesota to private parties. They list each parcel of land offered for sale in a given year or span of years and include both original sales and resales of forfeited or delinquent lands. If a parcel was not sold the first time it was offered, or if it later became forfeit or delinquent, it may be listed in more than one place. These volumes constitute an administrative record of transactions, not legal instruments conveying title.

The record for each parcel sold includes certificate number, legal description, appraised value per acre, value of improvements, name of occupant if preempted, total acreage, sale date, purchase price, amount paid at time of sale, unpaid balance, first year's interest, and purchaser's name. The records were kept by year or span of years, thereunder by county and location; those for 1862-1869 are further subdivided by land category within each county. The records for each county usually include a yearly recapitulation of sales. There are no records for some counties.

Finding Aids: Volumes for 1862-1872 are indexed by county.

Related Records: Continued by **Record of Sales: State Trust Fund Lands**, ca.1878-ca.1940 (below).

Record of Sales: State Trust Fund Lands, ca.1878-ca.1940. 6 rolls microfilm (15 vols.: 6.0 c.f.)

Continuation of **Record of Sales**, 1862-1879 (above), arranged alphabetically by county and thereunder by location or by land category and location. The records for land sections containing water, swamps, or railroad rights of way are usually accompanied by a plat drawing and occasionally by other supporting documentation. There are no records for some counties.

Related Records: **Memorandum of Sale of State Lands** (page 13). Continued by **Abstract of State Land** (page 8).

Record of Sales: State Trust Fund Lands (Supplement), ca.1883-ca.1936. 2.5 c.f. (7 vols.)

Summary records of the sale of state trust fund land in the five north-central Minnesota counties (Aitkin, Cass, Itasca, Koochiching, and St. Louis) in which heavy concentrations of trust fund lands were located, as well as in Dakota County. These volumes supplement the microfilmed series **Record of Sales: State Trust Fund Land** (ca.1878-ca.1940).

The volumes list each parcel of trust fund land offered for sale, including both original sales and resales of forfeited or payment-delinquent land. The record for each parcel sold includes the following information: certificate number, legal description of the tract, date of sale, appraised value per acre, cash required for timber on the tract, year appraised, purchase price per acre, principal paid at time of sale, unpaid balance, first year's interest, purchaser's name and address, and type of trust fund land. Toward the end of each volume are additional listings, apparently representing later appraisals, classifications, and sales of new parcels, as well as resales.

The microfilmed **Record of Sales** includes earlier versions of the volumes for each of these counties except Dakota. All sales entries recorded in the filmed volumes are also recorded in these volumes, in addition to updated entries. There is no volume for Dakota County in the filmed series.

Arrangement: By county, thereunder by range, township, and section, with some deviations.

School and Other State Land to be Offered for Sale: Published Lists, 1905-1914. 1 vol.

Newspaper clippings and flyers listing school lands and other state lands to be offered for public sale at designated places and times. Pasted into the volume chronologically by date of sale.

Special Certificate Record, 1870-1974. 1 roll microfilm (5 vols.: 1.0 c.f.)

Special certificates (nos. 1-889) issued to purchasers of forfeited land that had originally been sold as school, swamp, internal improvement, or other trust fund land. When a parcel of state land was sold, the purchaser was issued a certificate, which was a record of his or her interest in the land and which stated the conditions of the sale. When the sale conditions were met, the state issued a patent that formally transferred title to the land. If the certificate holder failed to satisfy the terms of the sale, through non-payment of principal and interest or of assessed taxes, the land reverted to the state, which could then resell it. Purchasers of such forfeited land were issued a "special certificate" that transferred the original certificate holder's interest in the land to the new purchaser.

Each certificate is a printed form filled in with special certificate number, category of state land, original purchaser, legal description of the property, total acreage, per acre purchase price, original certificate number and date issued, unpaid balance, statement of the grounds for foreclosure, date of resale, and new purchaser.

Arrangement: By chronologically assigned certificate number.

State Subdivisions Plat Book, undated. 1 roll microfilm (1 vol.: 0.5 c.f.)
Plat drawings of school lands (sections 16 and 36), salt spring lands, and several parcels of internal improvement lands, which were subdivided and sold in parcels of less than 40 acres. They show lot number and acreage of each subdivided parcel, roads and rights of way that cross it, and any rivers, lakes, swamps, or other natural features located in the section. Some plats also include surveyors' field notes and other documentation.

Finding Aids: The volume includes an index organized by range, town, and section.

State Subdivisions Plat Files, undated and 1862-1909. 0.2 c.f. (2 folders and 1 oversize folder)
Maps, field notes, and a few letters regarding the resurvey or platting of various parcels of state land, primarily school land. They supplement, and probably duplicate to a large extent, the **State Subdivisions Plat Book** (above).

State Trust Fund Land Certificates, 1862-1984. 79.0 c.f. (79 boxes)
After the final payment had been made on a parcel of state land, the purchaser turned in to the State Land Office the original certificate of purchase, along with documentation of any changes in ownership that might have occurred since the initial filing, and received title in the form of a land patent. This series consists of the certificates, annotated as needed to show conveyance to new owner(s) since their initial issuance, and often accompanied by such ancillary documents as abstracts of title, warranty and quitclaim deeds, probate court decrees, receipts for sale, certificates of assignment, and county auditors' certificates of taxes paid.

The patent number is written or typed onto the face of each certificate, and often (but not always) onto the accompanying documents as well. Several certificates may be encompassed in a single patent number. Some patent numbers are missing. The series ends with patent number 39894. Certificates for reform school land patents are not present.

Arrangement: By type of trust fund land and thereunder by patent number. Boxes 71, 72, and 79 contain documentation of related transactions. There is no known means of access by certificate number to this series.

Swamp Land Miscellaneous Lists and Correspondence, undated and 1862-1923. 1.6 c.f. (1 box and 2 partial boxes)
Lists of swamp lands in Minnesota Indian reservations (undated); miscellaneous correspondence and lists relating to the selection, approval, and patenting of state swamp lands; various lists and registers created during the process of resolving conflicting claims to swamp land tracts; and contest case files, containing letters and documents relating to contests of the state's claims to particular parcels of swamp land.

Swamp Land Patents: United States to Minnesota, 1865-1960. 2 rolls microfilm (4 vols.: 3.0 c.f.)

These patents record the transfer of title to designated swamp lands from the federal government to the state of Minnesota under congressional acts of September 28, 1850, and March 12, 1860. A single patent may include from one to over 100 individual parcels in several townships. Each patent records the patent or list number, land office through which it was issued, legal descriptions of the parcels patented, total acreage patented within each township, aggregate acreage in the entire patent, date the governor of Minnesota made application for the patent, and date the patent was executed.

The patents were at some point compiled into four volumes corresponding approximately to the four federal land districts existing in Minnesota in 1900: Duluth, St. Cloud, Crookston, and Marshall. Patents for the Cass Lake land district, which was established in 1903, are intermingled with the others. Within each volume the patents are arranged for the most part by individual land office, and thereunder by chronologically assigned patent number (list number after 1914).

Typed transcriptions were prepared for 185 pages that were abraded, faint, or otherwise unable to produce a sharp image when filmed. Each transcription is filmed immediately after the page that it transcribes.

Finding Aids: A consolidated index, arranged by location, refers to volume and page number; individual volume indexes are keyed to patent numbers.

Swamp Land Record, ca.1860-1931. 3 rolls microfilm (13 vols.: 4.5 c.f.)

An administrative record of the state of Minnesota's acquisition and disposition of swamp and overflowed lands. After the state surveyor general had identified and selected tracts of swamp land, they were patented from the federal government to the state, which then either sold the tracts, regranted them to railroads, or retained possession. The volume was apparently compiled in 1876, at which time prior transactions were recorded retrospectively.

Each volume contains records, by county, for individual counties or groups of contiguous counties; in several instances land in a given county appears in more than one volume. Within each volume the swamp land tracts are listed by range, town, section, and fractional section. The entry for each parcel gives legal description, acreage, date selected by the surveyor general, date patented to the state, by whom selected and to whom deeded from the state, other disposition (such as selection rejected or contested), and occasional remarks. Names of private parties to whom swamp lands were sold are not recorded, however; only the sale date appears in the "Remarks" column. Grantee railroads are indicated by stamped corporate initials, repeated in the "Remarks" column if the original stamps had faded excessively.

Finding Aids: Each volume is indexed by range and township; there is also a consolidated index.

Swamp Land Selection Lists, 1875-1915. 1.75 c.f. (11 vols. and 4 folders) Lists of swamp land selected by the state as compiled from the records of the U.S. Surveyor General's Office. The series lists all land selected by the state under terms of the Swamp Land Act of March 12, 1860. Annotations made by the registers and receivers of local land offices indicate any claims against the parcels existing at the time the selections were filed. Further notes by the State Land Office give the eventual disposition of the selected tracts.

Volumes 1-5 were compiled in 1875 and encompass all swamp selections on land surveyed prior to 1875. Later volumes were compiled periodically as the surveys of portions of the state were completed and selection lists were filed by the state.

Arrangement: By land district office through which the original selection lists were filed.

Finding Aids: Volumes and/or individual lists are indexed by range and township.

Related Records: **Approved Lists: Swamp Land** (page 11); **Swamp Land Record** (page 23). Also **U.S. Surveyor General: Swamp Land Lists** (page 54).

STATE AUDITOR
LAND DEPARTMENT RECORDS

Annual Reports of the Inspector of State Mines, 1904-1918. 0.3 c.f.

Annual reports (typewritten) of Frank A. Wildes, inspector of iron mines situated on state lands, to the state auditor. They review inspection and oversight work in general; comment on mining policies, problems, and prospects, and on relations with mining companies and the general public; and describe the activities of each operating mine and the general administration of the inspection office.

Reports for 1904-1906 are fairly brief; subsequent reports are longer and include lists of contracts and leases and statistics on ore production, reserve tonnages, and the like. The reports also comment on sand and gravel pits, squatters, waste dumping, and timber trespass on state mineral lands. The inspector and his assistants were headquartered in Hibbing. Reports for 1909-1910 are supplemented by Virginia district reports of August T. Koerner. Two versions of reports for 1904-1910 are present.

The report for 1917 is supplemented by reports of W. A. Deichen, chief engineer of the state mining department (1915-1917) and P. M. Ostrand, inspector of state mines on the Cuyuna Range (1917). Reports for 1911-1913 and 1915 are missing. A handwritten note on the 1918 report says: "See bound reports 1904 to 1923, incl. on shelves in the main office (March 14, 1924)."

Related Records: **Correspondence: Letters Sent, Superintendent of Mines** (page 26) contains Mineral Lands Division annual reports (1926-1932, carbon copies).

Correspondence, General, 1921-1939. 18.0 c.f. (18 boxes)

Most of the correspondence in this series concerns the disposition of state-owned lands to the public. There are inquiries about availability and prices of specific parcels for sale or lease; state land auction announcements and other information; and data regarding land and tax payments, as well as the issuance and transfer of land titles and the disposition of tax-delinquent lands. After April, 1933, the auditor's replies to land inquiries cite information received from the Conservation Department or refer the addressee to that agency for information.

Mixed with this correspondence are letters, unrelated to land business, that document such other matters handled by the state auditor's office as school district bonding and other bonds, property and inheritance tax matters, and warrants for various purposes.

Arrangement: Alphabetical by surname of correspondent, with letters received and sent interfiled. Folders of unsorted correspondence, dating largely from 1939, are filed at the end of the fully arranged materials for each letter.

Correspondence: Immigration Letters Sent, 1906-1911. 2 vols.

Letters of the state auditor regarding the availability and character of state lands, land sale dates and procedures, and the distribution of circulars and advertisements for state lands. Largely carbon copies.

Many of the letters are written to individuals in other states, often praising Minnesota as a desirable place to resettle, and to Minnesota newspapers, including the ethnic press, regarding the printing of land advertisements. The activities of Minnesota's Immigration Board are occasionally mentioned.

Related Records: **Correspondence with Hibbing Office** (page 27) contains similar correspondence (vol. 2, 1912-1916).

Correspondence: Land and Mineral Letters, 1875-1922. 1.0 c.f. (6 vols.)
Auditor's correspondence and memos concerning appraisal, sale, and lease of state lands; mineral leases, mining contracts, prospecting permits, royalties paid to the state, and similar matters relating to mining activities by companies and individuals on state lands; and a few miscellaneous aspects of the use of state lands. Letters for 1875-1899 (approximately 60 items) largely pertain to railroad rights of way across state lands.

Volumes 1-5 (1875-1915) consist almost entirely of incoming letters. In volume 6 (1917-1922), letters received and carbon copies of letters sent are intermingled.

Arrangement: Chronological. Although the volumes are sequentially numbered, there are gaps in the date spans of the letters.

Finding Aids: Each volume has an index to personal and corporate correspondents.

Correspondence: Letters Sent, Superintendent of Mines, 1921-1932. 4.8 c.f. (37 vols.)
Carbon copies of outgoing letters, memos, and agreements of Frank A. Wildes, superintendent of state mines, with some from other members of the mines department and from the state auditor. They largely concern sale and lease of state mineral and other lands, the operation of mines on state land, exploration and analysis of mineral resources, advertising of land sales and prospecting permits, and general administration and finances of the department of mines. However, many letters relate to management and recreational development of state lands in general, particularly to water resource management, dam construction, and riparian rights.

Primary recipients are officials and personnel of mining companies, personnel of the auditor's office and of the state mineral lands office in Hibbing, Minnesota newspapers, and members of the general public.

Copies of a few lengthy reports or articles on Minnesota's iron ores and mineral resources are also included. There are also copies of the annual reports of the mineral lands division (1926-1932), with detailed information on mining activities on state lands.

Arrangement: Chronological.

Finding Aids: Each volume contains an index to correspondents.

Related Records: **Correspondence with Hibbing Office** (page 27). **Conservation Department: Lands and Minerals Division: Director's Reading File** (page 34) is the direct successor to this series.

Correspondence: Mineral Department Letters, 1908-1914. 1.5 c.f. (9 vols.)
Auditor's correspondence regarding the granting, purchase, and transfer of mineral leases and mining contracts on state lands; annual or

quarterly royalty payments by mining companies and individuals; delinquencies in payment; and reporting of mining activities, ore production, and shipments (reports themselves are not included). A few letters concern Minnesota's mineral resources and mining industry in general.

Many of the letters from the auditor's office are to Frank A. Wildes, state inspector of mines. Wildes' letters to the auditor do not appear to be present in this series.

The assignment of mining contracts on state lands required approval by the state auditor (Revised Laws 1905 c40 s2493).

Arrangement: In two chronological subseries: letters received (each volume arranged internally by name of correspondent) and letters sent.

Related Records: **Land Letters** (pages 27-29) and **Correspondence: Land and Mineral Letters** (page 26).

Correspondence, Miscellaneous, 1881-1909. 0.25 c.f. (5 folders)

Letters received from W. E. Culkin, attorney for the state, regarding swamp land contests (1906-1909); letters received from the U.S. Army Corps of Engineers regarding state lands to be affected by proposed construction of flowage reservoirs on the Mississippi River (1881-1906); and miscellaneous letters received concerning land surveys, sales, and leases (1886-1904). This series may receive additional increments as more isolated units of correspondence are located.

Correspondence with Hibbing Office, 1912-1934. 3.0 c.f. (21 vols.)

Correspondence largely of the state auditor or deputy auditor with Frank A. Wildes, chief inspector (later superintendent) of mines and his deputies, headquartered at Hibbing; some is with mining companies, leaseholders, and other interested parties. It concerns the development, operation, and output of iron mines and occasionally other extractive activities on state lands; Wildes' oversight and inspection of these mines; general management of and income from the state's mineral lands and mining leases; and the administration, personnel, and expenses of the Hibbing office.

Early volumes include Wildes' detailed reports of his inspections of mines and mining properties. After about 1919-1920, these dwindle in number and detail, more of the correspondence is with the Hibbing office deputies and agents rather than with Wildes himself, and it pertains more to general leasing matters, logistics of the office's management, and transmittal of income and expenditures.

Arrangement: Volumes are numbered in a generally chronological sequence, although there are several aberrations.

Finding Aids: Most of the volumes include indexes to other correspondents.

Related Records: Companion series for post-1920 is **Correspondence: Letters Sent, Superintendent of Mines** (page 26).

Land Letters Received, 1870-1914. 6.9 c.f. (42 vols. and 1 folder)

Letters received by the auditor's office regarding all aspects of the administration of state (trust fund) lands, including ownership, transfer, purchase, payment, and use of school and swamp lands; land taxes and tax forfeitures; mineral leases, ore shipments, and royalties paid for mining done on state lands; stumpage and logging; railroad rights of way; and school district and municipal loans and bonds, as well as general fiscal matters regarding lands in the state, trust fund and otherwise.

The majority are letters of transmittal or requests for information, although many others are substantial. Correspondents include county auditors and treasurers transmitting purchase and tax data and receipts, as well as members of the general public and officers or representatives of land and logging companies, railroads, law firms, and other organizations.

All volumes are identified on their spines as "Land Letters." Their indexes often refer to them as "Land Dept." or "State Land Office" letters. Other variations in identification are noted on the volume list.

Each volume is internally paginated via a stamped number on each letter or page; however, some letters were skipped. Month and day dates on the spine titles are often inaccurate; where they were determined definitely to be inaccurate, the volume list gives only the inclusive year(s).

Arrangement: Volumes are numbered more or less chronologically. Letters within the volumes are bound alphabetically by first letter of county name and/or correspondent's surname, occasionally by date, and several in no readily discernible order.

Finding Aids: Each volume is indexed by name of correspondent, usually including county and/or corporate names also.

Related Records: This series, **Land Letters Sent**, and **Land Letters Received and Sent** constitute a single numbered set; volumes 38, 57, and 77 are missing. This set precedes and overlaps with **Correspondence, General,** 1921-1939 (page 25).

Land Letters Sent, 1873-1914. 4.5 c.f. (35 vols.)

Letterpress copies of outgoing letters of the state auditor as state land commissioner, regarding all aspects of the administration of state-owned lands and their disposition to the public, including purchase, payment, and transfers of title; land taxes and tax forfeitures; appraisals and reappraisals of state lands and the timber thereon; timber and grass cutting contracts and timber trespass (unauthorized cutting); and unsettled or contested titles. Letters during the 1870s and 1880s also deal with railroad land selections. Mineral leases, including many notifications of payments due on mining contracts, comprise a large proportion of the letters for ca.1903-ca.1908; and discussion of ditch assessments appears around 1910. Some letters deal with other aspects of the administration of the auditor's office.

Many are letters of transmittal, responses to queries from the public about land offerings and sales or the status of specific parcels, and various notifications and authorizations to county auditors and treasurers regarding taxation and land payment matters. Other recipients include the registers and receivers of U.S. district land offices in Minnesota, the commissioner of the U.S. General Land Office, officials of railroad and mining companies, and land appraisers.

All volumes are identified as "State Land Letters" or "Land Department Letters" unless otherwise noted on the volume list. Most of them were numbered and labeled, often inaccurately, some time after their creation; the volume list notes, in brackets, corrections to the original labels. Many of the pre-1900 letters are so faint as to be illegible.

Arrangement: Volumes are numbered in a general chronological progression, although with several gaps or overlaps in date spans, even where the volume numbers are consecutive. Letters within each volume are chronological, with some aberrations.

Finding Aids: Each volume is indexed by name of correspondent.

Land Letters Received and Sent, 1911-1930. 1.5 c.f. (10 vols.)

Correspondence concerning the administration of state-owned lands and their disposition to the public, including purchase and transfer of title, land taxes and tax forfeitures, mineral leases and royalties, municipal and school district loans and bonds, and related matters. Many are letters of transmittal, requests for information, and routine replies.

All volumes are identified on their spines as "Land Letters." Each volume is internally paginated via a stamped number on each letter or page.

Arrangement: Volumes are numbered in a general chronological progression. Letters within the volumes are usually bound alphabetically by first letter of county name or correspondent's surname. Incoming and outgoing letters are interfiled.

Finding Aids: Each volume is indexed by name of correspondent.

Letters Received from the General Land Office, 1874-1939. 2.5 c.f.

Letters and land lists relating to the selection, status, and transfer from the federal government to the state of various grant and trust fund lands. Most pertain to the state's claim to swamp and railroad lands and to conflicting or contested claims stemming from prior sale or homestead entry. They consist of letters and enclosures sent to the auditor and governor by the U.S. Secretary of the Interior and the commissioner of the U.S. General Land Office, letters from the district land offices in Minnesota, and notices and findings of contested claims.

Arrangement: In three subseries by source or document type; thereunder roughly chronological.

Finding Aids: Detailed series description.

Record of Deeds, ca.1851-1928. 5.0 c.f. (13 vols.)

Handwritten (vols. 1-12) and typed (1 vol.) copies of warranty deeds and some patents and related documents for lands acquired by the state of Minnesota for state institutions, normal schools, the University of Minnesota, public buildings, state parks and forests, highway easements, and miscellaneous properties.

A deed [?] number is usually recorded, but the deeds are not in numerical or any other readily discernible order. Most deeds have also been annotated with a penciled number. These numbers are consecutive in volumes 6-11, but apparently random in volumes 1-5. Neither set of numbers has been systematically linked with any other known record series, although the penciled numbers may correlate with the documents reproduced on the first several rolls of a set of security microfilm entitled "Record of State-Owned Land" (not described in this guide).

Related Records: An **Index to Deeds on State Property,** not described in this guide, appears to consist of lists of many or most of the deeds in volumes 1-5. However, it does not cite or index these volumes, and there is no known way to directly correlate lists and volumes.

Reports of Public and Railroad Lands Sold, 1865-1942. 4.6 c.f. (5 boxes)
Lists of lands sold to private parties and paid for in full, with title passing to the purchaser and with the lands, which prior to final entry were exempt from real estate taxes, becoming subject to taxation.

These lists were sent in the spring of each year to the state auditor by the various U.S. district land offices in Minnesota and by the land grant railroads. They consist of all final entries made during the previous year; in addition, the railroad lists include lands for which purchase contracts were made or canceled. From these lists, the state auditor compiled lists to be sent to the individual county auditors for entry on their tax rolls (Laws 1862 c62 s24; Laws 1878 c1 s118; Laws 1881 c10 s20). In 1943 this function was transferred to the Taxation Department (Laws 1943 c564).

Information recorded for each parcel of land: purchaser's name, legal description, acreage, and county. Certification statements by the federal or railroad land commissioner are usually written onto or appended to the lists. Letters of transmittal and other facilitative correspondence are also included, especially for the 1920s, when the tax or title status of several individual parcels are discussed.

The abstracts for several years appear to be incomplete. Many covering letters from railroads are missing the land lists to which the letters refer. Lists of Indian reservation and ceded Chippewa agricultural lands are present for 1905-1907.

Arrangement: For 1865-1899, by year, thereunder by land district or railroad; for 1913-1942, primarily by land district or railroad, thereunder chronological.

Related Records: Continued by **Taxation Department: Reports of Public and Railroad Lands Sold** (not described in this guide).

Squatter Department Reports, 1916-1922. 0.4 c.f. (6 folders)
Itemized lists, prepared quarterly, of income received from leases of state lands. The lists specify location, name of lessee, rental rate, amount due, amount paid, and trust fund into which the money received was to be paid. They are accompanied by occasional information on the status of particular leases. Reports are present for the first to the third quarters of each year. The reports were compiled by the state squatter agent (Lisle E. Moody and A. E. Allen), sent to state superintendent of mines Frank A. Wildes, and by him to the state auditor.

Arrangement: Chronological.

Related Records: Some lists of leases are in **Superintendent of Mines Subject Files** (page 31).

Superintendent of Mines Subject Files, 1921-1932. 6.0 c.f. (6 boxes)

Office files of Frank A. Wildes, superintendent of state mines. Wildes, headquartered in St. Paul, was responsible for administering the state's program of mineral leases, inspection and oversight of mining operations, minerals research and analysis, and general management of mineral lands as well as of state lands in general.

His files focus on iron mining activities on Minnesota's Iron Range, including information on current mineral leases and prospecting permits, ore production and shipments, valuation, royalty payments, status of operations at the various mines, and iron ore analyses. There is some information on other minerals or on attempts to locate them, including gold (especially Vermilion River Mines, Inc.), copper, titanium, marl, sulphur, manganese, and peat. The files include numerous memoranda and reports from staff of the department's Hibbing office, particularly office head Dennis C. Bow and chief engineer Raymond J. Moore, with some from general inspector R. A. Mitchell, state squatter agent Albert E. Allen, and others. Several files contain historical information on Minnesota iron mines and mining.

Wildes' responsibilities involved other aspects of state lands administration as well, and he appears to have cultivated a personal interest in conservation of natural resources in general. His files contain information on surface leases of various sorts (sand and gravel, hay, rights of way, power pole lines, billboards, hunting cabins, muskrat farms); examination and leasing of lake shore lands; use of state waters; general land ownership and timber matters; a few specific land sales or transfers; dams, water levels, and water power development on boundary waters lakes, particularly Gabbro and Bald Eagle; and surveys and ownership determinations for unsurveyed islands.

There are data on lands and minerals staff, budget, property, offices, and research facilities; copies of attorney general opinions relating to land and mineral matters; and correspondence regarding exhibits of Minnesota's mineral resources prepared for county and state fairs. A few folders found with the 1921 files contain items of earlier date. A number of typescript articles, most apparently written by Wildes, discuss iron ores, other mineral resources, and conservation issues in general.

Scattered throughout the files are photographs of mining operations and buildings, lakes, and related areas; and blueprint sketch maps of mine sites and of the locations of various types of leases and rights of way.

Arrangement: Within each year, by office file number.

Related Records: Succeeded by **Conservation Department: Lands and Minerals Division: Director's Subject Files** (pages 34-35); companion series is **Conservation Department: Lands and Minerals Division: Mine Inspection Files** (not described in this guide).

Timber Records

The state auditor's office also amassed a large body of records relating to the appraisal and sale of timber on state land, ca.1865-1933. They include appraisers' field notes and reports, state land examiners' reports and miscellany, logging permits and bonds, reports of timber cut under permits, correspondence regarding timber and state stumpage land, stumpage sale registers of various types, and registers of timber trespass (illicit logging) cases. The majority of these records are unprocessed.

Other Land Department Records

Isolated files or file units concerning state lands may be located as other records are processed, and some occasionally are transferred from the DNR Land Bureau. They are currently (1985) grouped into several tentatively titled series: "Miscellaneous Correspondence and Reports," "Miscellaneous Timber Files," and "Miscellaneous Land Files." Some may correlate with or duplicate other series in the auditor's office or the Conservation Department. They comprise a variety of correspondence, typescript and published reports, statistical compilations, legal documents, memoranda, pamphlets, and other materials pertaining to the management and use of the state's timber and mineral lands. A few files relate to swamp and grass lands, lake property, state parks, and other land holdings. Also among them are railroad right of way files, miscellany concerning Indian allotments and reservations, information on land-related organizations and development activities and on the state's land exchange program, a list of railroad selections (1880-1925), a reappraisal of Chippewa pine lands (1889), and mining company reports (1913-1932).

OTHER RECORDS OF THE STATE AUDITOR

Since management of the state's lands, the resources thereon, and the income therefrom constituted a substantial component of the state auditor's duties until 1931, a number of other records that are not specifically linked to the Land Department/State Land Office nevertheless include considerable land-related information.

Annual and Biennial Reports
They deal at some length with the auditor's activities as land commissioner, including comments on the status of land surveys and selections, land sales and sale procedures, mineral and other leases, and problems and accomplishments in the transfer and management of state lands, with statistics on land appraisals, selections, and sales, timber harvested, ore mined, income and disbursements of the various trust funds, and related data.

Attorney General's Opinions, 1883-1931. 4 folders.
Opinions of the attorney general's office, in the form of letters received by the auditor, relating to various fiscal and land management responsibilities of the auditor.

Fiscal Department: General Correspondence, 1858-1931. ca.80 c.f.
Several series of letterbooks and correspondence relating to financial matters include some letters concerning management of state lands, land sales, and receipts therefrom. These series have not been analyzed in detail for subject content. Some of the auditor's correspondence and subject files after 1931 also pertain to land sales.

Fiscal Department: Miscellaneous Records
The largely unprocessed records of the Fiscal Department include scattered volumes of accounts related specifically to the sale or lease of state trust fund lands, primarily before 1900. They include interest reductions, payments to land appraisers, income and expenses of various trust funds and land acquisition accounts, accounts for the sale of stumpage on state lands, abstracts of land sales, and a variety of other receipts and disbursements connected with state lands. The auditor's records also include several series or files documenting loans made to school districts, counties, and municipalities from the state's permanent trust funds; the bonded indebtedness covered by these loans; and investment of trust funds.

CONSERVATION DEPARTMENT
LANDS AND MINERALS DIVISION RECORDS

Director's Reading File, 1933-1967. 58.0 c.f. (58 boxes)

Bound carbon copies of outgoing letters and memos from the St. Paul office of the Division of Lands and Minerals. The majority were written by or for divisional directors Frank A. Wildes (1933-July 1937) and Ray D. Nolan (August 1937 - June 1967). They are written to other division and department officials and employees, to the staff of the division's Hibbing office, to county auditors and other local officials, to other state agency officials, to mining companies, and to members of the general public. Letters for January-March, 1933, are from Wildes as superintendent of state mines, prior to the organization of the division. Beginning in 1940, an increasing number of letters are written by subordinate office personnel, especially the deputy division director and the state land agent.

The letters relate to all aspects of the management and disposition of state-owned lands and their mineral and timber resources. General land letters concern land sale activities, procedures, and advertising; responses to requests for information about state-owned land, especially about land available for sale or lease, the status of specific land parcels (especially tax-delinquent land), and lands available for homestead; procedures for payment on land purchases; and stumpage available for sale. Mineral letters focus on the iron ore lands of the Mesabi Range and discuss leases of mineral lands, payments thereon, the status of various mines, applications for prospecting permits, royalty payments, transmittal of reports from mining companies, and responses to public inquiries on ore lands and ore production. Other letters concern the general administration and personnel of the division.

Also included are copies of reports on ore properties; some detailed letters and reports to members of the state Executive Council on the status of land in various areas; instructions to field employees, appraisers, and mine inspectors; texts of some articles; and synopses of laws. From 1933 into the 1940s, many of Wildes' and Nolan's monthly divisional reports to the conservation commissioner are present.

Arrangement: Chronological. For 1933-1934, divided into subseries for land letters and mineral letters.

Finding Aids: Each volume contains an index to correspondents.

Related Records: Preceded by **Auditor: Land Department: Correspondence: Letters Sent, Superintendent of Mines** (page 26). Succeeded by **Natural Resources Department: Minerals Division: Reading File** (pages 38-39).

Director's Subject Files, 1933-1934. 2.0 c.f. (2 boxes)

Office files of Frank A. Wildes. They reflect the creation of the Division of Lands and Minerals within the newly established Conservation Department, the transfer of staff and functions from the state auditor's office, and the formulation or confirmation of policies and procedures for managing state-owned lands and mineral resources.

The files provide information on the organization, administration, staff, budget, and office equipment of the new division and its branch office in Hibbing; leases of state land and lake front property for various purposes; sale of tax-delinquent lands; iron mining on state lands, including mineral leases, ore shipments, stockpiling, ore analyses, royalties, and the status of operations at the various mines; gold ore leases, prospecting permits, and exploration work done, especially by Vermilion River Mines, Inc.; assorted other state land management, minerals, and general conservation matters; exhibits of Minnesota resources at county and state fairs; and a variety of projects funded in 1934 by the state Civil Works Administration. They include monthly or periodic reports of Wildes (to the conservation commissioner), chief mining engineer Raymond J. Moore, chief inspector D. A. Mitchell, and mining research engineer Withers Clay.

Although responsibility for lands and minerals activities was transferred from the state auditor to the Conservation Department when it was created in 1931, formal transfer of functions and personnel was not completed until April 1, 1933. Files for January-March, 1933, are from Wildes' service as superintendent of mines in the auditor's office.

Arrangement: Within each year, by office file number.

Related Records: Preceded by **Auditor: Land Department: Superintendent of Mines Subject Files** (page 31); succeeded by **Director's Subject Files**, 1935-1970 (unprocessed and not described in this guide). Companion series is **Conservation Department: Lands and Minerals Division: Mine Inspection Files** (also unprocessed and not described in this guide).

Mines and Mining Records

Approximately 20 cubic feet of unprocessed files pertain to mining activities on state-owned lands by private corporations acting as lessees or operating agents. They consist largely of ore royalty shipment reports and correspondence, showing tonnages of iron ore shipped from each mine and royalties paid to the state on the ore, and mine inspection files, comprising reports, correspondence, and compiled data on mines and their operation, mining companies, and iron ore production, assay, stockpiling, and shipments.

Other Records

An assortment of unprocessed Lands and Minerals Division records pertain to specific projects or other aspects of the acquisition and management of state lands, including sets of abstracts of title for specific acquisition projects; scattered records or summaries of lease payments; appraisal or project files for individual acquisition, exchange, or flood control projects; and files on mining activities involving public waters. The provenance of some of these records has not been confirmed; records transferred to the State Archives from the Conservation Department's Forestry Division and Waters Division have often been found to interfile with those received from the Lands and Minerals Division.

OTHER CONSERVATION DEPARTMENT RECORDS

Commissioner's Office: General Correspondence, 1937-1970. 105.0 c.f.
Alphabetical subject/correspondence files for each year or biennium, concerning all aspects of the administration, activities, and interests of the Conservation Department. Among them are files on the Lands and Minerals and Forestry divisions, land acquisition, land exchange, tax-delinquent and tax-forfeited lands, land sales, mining activities on state lands, land for state parks and reserves, and public land law review (especially in 1967-1968). There are occasional files on such matters as timber contracts, lieu land selections for state trust fund lands (1949-1950), conservation lands, county and state ditches, land ownership studies, state lands in various counties, and the U.S. Bureau of Land Management. Files specific to land matters appear to decrease in frequency in the 1960s.

Commissioner's Office: Monthly and Quarterly Reports, 1935-1942. 4.0 c.f. (4 boxes)
Reports of the commissioner of conservation to the Conservation Commission, including reports from the directors of divisions. Those from the Lands and Minerals Division review land sales, land appraisal work, policies for management and resale of payment-delinquent and tax-delinquent lands, minerals research, oversight of mining activities on state lands, and status of work at individual iron mines and other mineral leaseholdings. Reports from the department's other divisions include frequent references to the acquisition of land for state parks, state forests, wildlife management areas, and game refuges.

Forestry Division Records, 1931-1971. 300.0 c.f.
The records of this division pertain to all aspects of the protection, management, improvement, and use of state-owned forest lands, as well as the division's role in promoting silviculture and forest conservation on private lands. They include files on land acquisition and its incorporation into state parks, state and national forests, memorial forests, and game refuges; land and timber surveys and appraisals; land classification; timber cutting regulations, logging permits, auction sales, and timber trespass (illicit logging) on state lands; acquisition or sale of tax-forfeited lands; land exchange programs; land use planning; leases and permits for use of state lands; and photographs of state forest lands.

Several files continue or encompass records of the formerly autonomous Forestry Board. A number of other subject files include items that pre-date the existence of the Conservation Department. Some records are found as Lands and Forestry Division, which was created in 1967 with a merger of the Forestry Division and the Lands Section of the former Lands and Minerals Division.

Game and Fish Division Records
Included in the records of this division are files concerning lands acquired and developed as wildlife management areas, conservation reserves, wetlands, and game refuges. Most are incorporated into the subject files maintained by various divisional staff and sub-units.

Parks and Recreation Division Records

These files include scattered data on land acquisition for state parks, land exchange for the Superior National Forest, land use planning, and data on individual state parks.

NATURAL RESOURCES DEPARTMENT RECORDS

In 1971 the name of the Conservation Department was changed to the Department of Natural Resources (Laws 1969 c1129). The new department continued the operational divisions of its predecessor: Game and Fish; Lands and Forestry; Parks and Recreation; Waters, Soils, and Minerals; and Field Services and Enforcement. During the period from 1972 to 1974, the department underwent a reorganization aimed at decentralizing its operations. One result of this process was to create a Bureau of Land to coordinate all land activities of the department, including land acquisition and supervision of the leasing and sale of state lands.

Many of the operational files of the Natural Resources Department are still in the department's custody. The State Archives does, however, hold a substantial body of correspondence and subject files of the commissioner's office and various subordinate units. They include a modest amount of information on state land matters.

Commissioner's Office: Correspondence and Subject Files, 1971-1981. 63.0 c.f.
Several sets of alphabetical or numerical subject/correspondence files, supplemented by reading files of outgoing letters, concerning all aspects of the administration, activities, and interests of the Natural Resources Department, kept by the commissioner and deputy commissioner. They include files on land resources, "land control," land acquisition and exchange, land sales and leases, land use classification, ditches, mining and mineral resources on state lands, timber sales, the divisions of Lands and Forestry and Waters, Soils, and Minerals, and various specific parks, forests, and sites.

Minerals Division: Reading File, 1967-1976 (bulk 1969-1972). 0.8 c.f. (1 box and 1 vol.)
Carbon copies of outgoing letters regarding the management of mineral resources on state-owned lands, particularly the iron ore lands of the Mesabi Range. They concern leases of mineral lands, royalty payments, the status of various mining operations, responses to public inquiries on ore lands and mining, and management and personnel of the Minerals Division in general. A few letters, although written by divisional staff, concern tax-forfeited lands and the rent and royalties received from them, as well as other general matters regarding state-owned land; these may, however, all concern mineral lands as well.

From July, 1967, to June, 1975, the letters are those of the Minerals Section of the Waters, Soils, and Minerals Division (formerly the Lands and Minerals Division) of the Conservation Department (1967-1970) and the Natural Resources Department. During this period, some were written by division director Eugene R. Gere or his administrative assistant, others by Minerals Section personnel directly or for Gere, and a number by chief mining engineer Elwood F. Rafn. A few are from the DNR commissioner's office. In July, 1975, a separate Minerals

Division was formed with Rafn as director, and subsequent letters are from him or his staff.

Arrangement: Chronological.

Finding Aids: Letters 1967-1971 include indexes to correspondents.

Related Records: Preceded by **Conservation Department: Lands and Minerals Division: Director's Reading File** (page 34).

GOVERNOR'S OFFICE RECORDS

Executive Journals, 1858-1915. 11 vols.
These constitute a record of official acts of, and documents received and sent by, the governor. Early journals, especially those for 1858-1864 (2 vols.), include records of official actions and copies of outgoing letters regarding the selection and title transfers of trust fund, railroad, and salt spring lands.

Executive Journal: Railroad Matters, 1858-1863. 1 vol.
Contains copies of documents, or notations concerning the filing of documents, relating to railroads, primarily the conveyance of deeds, bonds, liens, and certifications of completion in connection with the construction of the rail lines.

Governor's Records, 1858-1888.
The governor's records for this period contain a variety of individual files on land-related matters, particularly annual files for lands and railroads in general (usually one or two folders per year), but also including some individual folders for salt spring lands, university and school lands, swamp lands, correspondence with the U.S. Interior Department and General Land Office, and occasional files for particular railroads or land controversies. After 1889, most such files were kept by the governor's office as a single consolidated **Railroad and Land Matters File** (below).

Railroad and Land Matters File, 1885-1915 (bulk 1889-1900). 1.0 c.f.
Correspondence, notes, deeds, lists of lands, legal and court documents, and related materials centering on aspects of the ownership and conveyance of state trust fund and railroad grant lands that were handled by or routed through the governor's office. A large proportion of the file deals with relinquishments of swamp and other lands previously settled or claimed by private parties. A majority of the railroad matters involve the St. Paul, Minneapolis and Manitoba Railway and its successor, the Great Northern, but other railroads are also represented. Other documents in the file concern the 1893-1894 pinelands investigation, terms and conditions of railroad land grants, and salt spring selections (1891).

Governor's Records, 1900-1931.
Substantive documentation on railroad and land matters ceases to be present in the records of the governor's office after about 1900. Scattered files pertain to tax-forfeited lands, land appraisal, ditches, mines and mineral lands, and miscellaneous matters, mainly prior to 1920. There may also be some data in correspondence and subject files relating to the state auditor, drainage, forestry, national forests, and the U.S. Interior Department.

Governor's Records, 1932-1982.
Minor land-related files appear in the governor's executive letters or general files for most years, primarily under the file titles "Land

Exchange Commission," "Conservation Department: Land and Minerals," and "Natural Resources" (various files). They consist largely of correspondence with and informational copies from these and occasionally other agencies, concerning such matters as transmittal of swamp land and right of way deeds, actions of the Land Exchange Commission/Board, mineral leases and mining operations, sale of highway right of way and access parcels, transferrals of tax-forfeited land, and miscellaneous aspects of the management and disposition of state-owned land. A scattering of land-related data is also found among the files of various staff members in the offices of governors Wendell Anderson, Rudy Perpich, and Al Quie (1971-1982). Other information includes a land acquisition study file among the records of the Governor's Task Force on Waste and Mismanagement, 1977-1978 (Perpich); and various file segments relating to Reserve Mining Company, copper-nickel, peat, and other mining development on Iron Range lands.

Letters Sent (Letterpress), 1889-1916. 36 rolls microfilm (77 vols.) Among these largely routine outgoing letters from the governor's office are some relating to railroad and swamp land grants (vols. 3, 16, 18), complaints about timber trespass (vols. 48-52), and resignations of state land appraisers (vols. 73-74).

SECRETARY OF STATE RECORDS

Official Letters, Communications, and Railroad Liens, 1856-1942. 5.0 c.f.
Records of and indexes to documents received for filing in the secretary of state's office, some of which were recorded (copied) into volumes and others of which were filed as loose items. A number of them, especially 1857-1870, concern the incorporation and construction of land grant and other railroads, including various tax and legal matters, liens held by private parties for construction costs, mortgages and trust deeds, construction bonds, reports and certifications of construction work done, and non-payment by railroads for rights of way. Many of the documents are addressed to the governor.

Railroad Records, 1857-1972. 46.5 c.f.
Copies of deeds of trust, mortgages, indentures, leases, agreements, and other instruments filed by land grant and other railroad companies with the secretary of state. They consist of General Railroad Records (39 vols.), indexes for 1857-1917 (2 vols.), and separate volumes for the St. Paul, Minneapolis and Manitoba, St. Paul and Duluth, Minnesota Valley, Hastings and Dakota, St. Paul and Pacific, and St. Paul and Sioux City railways. Most do not relate directly to individual land holdings.

Annual Reports
The report for 1882 contains cumulative indexes to books of official letters, communications, and railroad liens and books of railroad records. From 1883 to 1886, the reports list annual additions to these filings.

Maps, 1850s-1920. 4.5 c.f.
United States survey and military road survey maps, maps of railroad surveys and completed construction, and miscellaneous maps filed with the secretary of state. They are individually listed in the secretary of state's "Index to Railroad Records and Steamboats" (filed with **Railroad Records**, above). For the reports and certifications of completion that accompanied these maps, see: **Secretary of State: Official Letters . . .**, and **Governor: Executive Journals** and various land and railroad files.

OTHER LAND-RELATED RECORDS OF STATE AGENCIES

Administration Department

Records of the state Department of Administration include biennial budgets and budget requests from the departments of Conservation and Natural Resources, including their land management functions; a variety of correspondence and subject files that, among many other topics, refer to the acquisition, conveyance, disposition, and management of state-owned lands; and records of the 1955-1960 Minnesota Self-Survey, which reviewed the functions and operations of state agencies, including the Conservation Department's Lands and Minerals Division.

Attorney General

Various series of case files, correspondence files, and subject files contain information on contested school and swamp lands; Indian allotments and reservations; condemnations of land for state parks and forests and for other public facilities and purposes; miscellaneous land title matters; damages to state and private lands from flooding caused by power company dams on the Rainy River; acquisition of lands and easements, and subsequent damage claims, in connection with the Lac qui Parle Flood Control Project of the 1930s and 1940s; and the attorney general's participation on the Land Exchange Commission.

Drainage Commission

The records of the Drainage Commission (1897-1919) and its predecessor, the Red River Valley Drainage Commission, document drainage and flood control needs in the state in the early twentieth century, and the construction and maintenance of state-funded drainage ditches. They include a few reports and extensive field notes on hydrologic surveys throughout Minnesota. Many of the lands encompassed by the commission's interest were state-owned swamp and other tracts.

Economic Development Department

The commissioner's office subject files (1947-1980s) include some files on copper and nickel mining, iron ore and taconite mining, mineral rights, and land exchange, as well as a variety of other natural resources development issues and organizations with implications for state-owned lands in northern Minnesota.

Executive Council

The records of the Executive Council include a variety of files on such topics as land acquisition, mining and prospecting permits and contracts, land leases and sales, timber sales and permits, and flood control and development projects on state-owned lands, particularly with regard to state loans, expenditures, and other fiscal concerns.

Finance Department

Finance Department records include biennial budgets and budget proposals (1973-1983) and legislative files relating to fiscal matters, including those affecting the Natural Resources Department.

Forestry Board

The records of the Forestry Board and its predecessors (primarily 1895-1927) include information on the management of Minnesota's forest reserves, conservation and tree planting endeavors on state lands, fire prevention and control, and the administration of state parks.

Highway Department

There are scattered files on land, gravel and borrow pits, and rights of way owned, acquired, or leased by the department.

Immigration Board

Biennial reports (1867-1886 in MHS Library; 1908-1922 in State Archives) include information on land available and land sold for homesteads. The few items of correspondence (1911) pertain to disputed land titles and inquiries about homestead lands.

Investment Board

The board's correspondence, minutes, and financial records (1917-1957, ca.30 c.f.) document its investment and income management of state funds, including those derived from the sale of trust fund lands. The majority have not been analyzed for subject content.

Iron Range Resources and Rehabilitation Board

The records of this board, created in 1943 to encourage the development of the natural resources of northeastern Minnesota's Iron Range and to assist economic expansion in general in that area, include extensive files on peat and minerals research and mining programs, mineland reclamation, forestry, dams and waterways, and a variety of resource, economic, and tourism development activities, many involving state-owned land. There are some files on land ownership and on a project to relocate section corner posts in several northern counties. Some of these records are housed in the Iron Range Research Center, Chisholm.

Land Exchange Board

The Land Exchange Board, created in 1939, approves the exchange of lands owned by the United States government or private interests for state-owned lands. Its records (6 c.f.) consist of minutes, case files on specific land exchange transactions, and general information and subject files. A companion set of Land Exchange Reading Files is found with the records of the **Conservation Department: Forestry Division: State Land Management Section** (not described separately in this guide).

Legislative Commission on Minnesota Resources

The commission's minutes and subject files (1957-1978) contain a variety of information on the acquisition, use, and management of state lands, forests, waters, parks, and mineral resources, and of Voyageurs National Park land.

Legislature

In addition to voluminous general files of bills, journals, and committee minutes for both the senate and the house of representatives, there are scattered committee and subcommittee minutes and/or reports relating specifically to the public domain (house, 1921-ca.1963, and senate, 1941 or earlier to 1970), iron ore and peat lands (senate, 1921), forest resources and forest land ownership (interim, 1959-1961), and state lands (house, 1969-1970); and a few items relating to special investigating committees on Chippewa pine lands (1874) and state timber and mineral lands (1907).

Lieutenant Governor

The files of lieutenant governors Rudy Perpich (1971-1976) and Lou Wangberg (1977-1981) include scattered data on state-owned lands and their resources, particularly iron ore and other mining matters.

Planning Board

Its records, among which are a large number of maps, plats, and reports, are largely unprocessed. They include data on ownership, characteristics, management, and use of Minnesota's public land and water resources.

Public Service Commission

Its records and those of its predecessor, the Railroad and Warehouse Commission, include a scattering of historical data on railroad rights of way, land grants, and land sales, as well as railroad valuation records that give some data on land holdings.

Revenue Department: Minerals Division

Records include abstracts of mineral reports of Minnesota iron mines (1942-1980), ad valorem tax reports from mining companies (1970-1978), and a variety of other activity and taxation data for companies mining iron and other ores on Minnesota land.

Surveyor General of Logs and Lumber

Between 1854 and 1967, this office was in charge of scaling all timber cut on state lands, surveying standing timber prior to sale, and acting as an arbitrator in scaling matters between private parties when requested to do so. Its records, which are inventoried but otherwise unprocessed, include a variety of scaling records and reports, timber sale billings and accounts, timber sale and logging permits, stumpage sale records, tally books, log journals and ledgers, log mark registers, correspondence, contracts, and miscellany. A number of record books pertain to timber cut by individual lumber companies. The office was abolished in 1967 and its duties transferred to the Conservation Department. Some surveyors' records are found with that department's Lands and Forestry Division files.

Tax Commission

The Tax Commission was created in 1907 and succeeded by the Taxation Department (now the Revenue Department) in 1939. Among its records are ore estimates from Minnesota iron mines (1909-1941, succeeded by records in the Revenue Department) and maps of the Mesabi Range.

Taxation Department: Mining Section

Its records consist of approximately 70 cubic feet of files on ore and tonnage valuation, ad valorem tax, equalization of mines and mineral properties, occupation taxes, present worth calculations, and royalty taxes for mining activity on Minnesota lands.

Territorial Records

Scattered letters in the files of the territorial governors (1849-1858) concern land office appointments, land sales and occupancy, selection of university lands, and related matters.

Timber Commissioners Board

The board, composed of the governor, state auditor (land commissioner), and state treasurer, was formed in 1895 in response to a scathing report on timber sale fraud submitted to the legislature the previous year by the Pine Lands Investigating Committee. It issued permits to cut timber on state lands in accordance with stringent appraisal provisions, received settlements for other authorized cutting, determined and penalized timber trespass, and coordinated with the Surveyor General of Logs and Lumber to appraise the logs actually harvested. Its minutes (incomplete) and examination and appraisal records document these functions during the period of its existence (1895-1925). Related timber files are found primarily among the records of the state auditor's office.

Treasurer

Records of the treasurer's office include a variety of registers, ledgers, other account books, and correspondence files documenting the receipt, distribution, and management of funds received from the sale and lease of state lands or the resources thereon, particularly receipts for and loans made from the permanent school fund and other trust funds, investment of these funds, and receipts from the sale of stumpage. There are also a few miscellaneous deed records. The majority of the treasurer's office records are unprocessed.

U.S. SURVEYOR GENERAL OF MINNESOTA

The Office of Surveyor General of Minnesota was established in 1857 and was responsible for conducting the original government survey of the public domain in the territory and state of Minnesota. The surveyor general's primary duties were awarding contracts for the survey of specified tracts, supervising the field work of the deputy surveyors, preparing official plats and descriptive lists for each township from the field notes of the deputy surveyors, and managing the accounts of the office.

Congress created the position of surveyor general by an act of 1796 establishing the "Office of Surveyor General Northwest of the Ohio" and "Office of Surveyor General Southwest of the Ohio." The surveyors general originally served directly under the secretary of the treasury. In 1836 the supervision of the federal survey was placed under the jurisdiction of the General Land Office (GLO), then a bureau within the Treasury Department. The surveyors general became direct subordinates of the commissioner of the GLO although they continued to operate independently of the local GLO land offices.

As westward expansion proceeded and the survey of older areas was completed, Congress authorized the creation of new survey districts and the relocation of surveyor general's headquarters within the old districts. The Office of Surveyor General of Minnesota was a lineal descendant of the Office of Surveyor General Northwest of the Ohio. That office had been located successively at: Marietta, Ohio, 1797-1804; Vincennes, Indiana, 1804-1805; Cincinnati, Ohio, 1805-1814; Chillicothe, Ohio, 1814-1829; Cincinnati, 1829-1845; and Detroit, Michigan, 1845-1857.

An act of Congress of March 3, 1857, instructed the Secretary of the Interior "to cause the Office of Surveyor General Northwest of the Ohio to be removed [from Detroit] to St. Paul in the Territory of Minnesota." The Detroit office was closed May 11, 1857. In a letter of May 23, 1857, surveyor general C. L. Emerson reported that "notes, maps, papers, documents and furniture" had arrived in St. Paul from Detroit and that he "would soon be ready to conduct such field work as may be ordered."[1]

The earliest surveys of land in Minnesota were conducted under the jurisdiction of the Surveyor General of Iowa and Wisconsin, headquartered at Dubuque, Iowa. These surveys, completed between 1848 and May, 1857, were primarily on land located between the St. Croix and Mississippi rivers or in the southeastern corner of Minnesota.

---

1. C. L. Emerson to Thomas Hendricks, GLO commissioner. USSG Letters Sent, Vol. J, p. 337.

After the establishment of the Office of Surveyor General of Minnesota, copies of the field notes, plats, and other records relevant to these surveys were transferred from Dubuque to St. Paul.

The government survey, sometimes referred to as the "congressional," "federal," or "rectangular" survey, divided the state into a grid of townships, each six miles square. The federal survey was based on a series of north-south principal meridians and east-west base lines. Survey points were measured from these base lines and principal meridians, giving each township a unique location north of a base line and west or east of a principal meridian. Each township was subdivided into 36 sections of 640 acres, quarter sections of 160 acres, and quarter-quarter sections of 40 acres.

Because part of Minnesota had belonged to the Northwest Territory and part to the Louisiana Territory, land in the state was subject to two different surveys. Land east of the Mississippi was platted under a survey originating on the "Galena" base line (near the Wisconsin-Illinois border) and was controlled by the 4th principal meridian. The survey of land west of the Mississippi commenced on a base line running through Clarendon, Arkansas, and was controlled by the 5th principal meridian. Townships east of the river are numbered 22-70 north of the Galena base line. Townships west of the Mississippi are numbered 101-164 north of the Clarendon base line.

Congress annually appropriated money for survey work in Minnesota. The surveyor general and the commissioner of the GLO decided which tracts were to be surveyed in a given fiscal year. Contracts for survey work were awarded to deputy surveyors by competitive bid. The deputy surveyor, with a crew of chainmen, axemen, and a compassman, ran the survey lines in the field and was responsible for erecting survey monuments, blazing trees, and recording all measurements in his field notes. The surveyor general verified the accuracy and completeness of the deputy surveyor's work and then submitted copies of the field notes and plats to the commissioner of the GLO for approval.

The Office of Surveyor General of Minnesota continued in operation until December, 1907, when the survey of Minnesota was essentially complete. After 1907 the commissioner of the GLO served, _ex officio_, as Surveyor General of Minnesota, and questions relating to the survey were forwarded to the GLO. A congressional act of 1940 provided that the records of the Office of Surveyor General of Minnesota be turned over to the Minnesota secretary of state.

The records of the U.S. Surveyor General of Minnesota, most of which were transferred to the State Archives from the secretary of state's office in 1966, include deputy surveyors' field notes (copies) and related records, surveyor general's office correspondence and accounts, contracts for surveys, township survey plats, and miscellaneous related records. The original survey field notes and plats remain (1985) in the custody of the Minnesota secretary of state's office. The University of Minnesota holds a microfilm copy of the field notes and plats sent to the commissioner of the GLO.

List of Surveyors General of Minnesota:

Charles L. Emerson, March 24, 1857-April 13, 1861
William Drew Washburn, April 13, 1861-May 15, 1865
Levi Nutting, May 15, 1865-May 18, 1869
Chester E. Davis, May 18, 1869-Dec. 8, 1870 (died in office)
C. T. Brown, Feb. 7, 1871-Oct. 13, 1873
Dana E. King, Oct. 1873-April 30, 1875
James Heaton Baker, May 1, 1875-April 4, 1879
J. H. Stewart, April 14, 1879-May 2, 1883
Martin Chandler, May 2, 1883-April 2, 1887
John Freeman Norrish, April 2, 1887-April 22, 1891
James Compton, April 22, 1891-Nov. 27, 1895
Patrick H. Kirwan, Nov. 27, 1895-Feb. 6, 1900
Eli S. Warner, Feb. 7, 1900-Dec. 30, 1907

RECORDS OF THE U.S. SURVEYOR GENERAL

Accounting Records, 1850-1907. 0.8 c.f. (3 vols. and 10 folders)
Quarterly accounts of survey appropriations received and of expenditures for salaries, survey work, and incidental expenses by the St. Paul surveyor general's office, supplemented by vouchers that give additional details on expenses or that document work not itemized in the quarterly accounts. They include monthly or quarterly payrolls (incorporated into the accounts), expenses for surveying the Red Lake Indian Reservation, accounts for the surveyor general's office at Detroit, Michigan (1850-1857), and accounts of the surveyor general as federal timber agent.

Arrangement: By record type or format; roughly chronological thereunder.

Related Records: **Surveyors' Accounts.**

Contracts for Surveys, 1857-1907. 1.4 c.f. (10 folders and 2 vols.)
Contracts between the surveyor general and deputy surveyors for the survey of specified tracts of public land (1881-1907, 10 folders), and a record of contracts awarded and special instructions issued (1857-1907, 2 vols.). They include contracts awarded at bid and "special instructions" from the General Land Office (GLO) and surveyor general to deputy surveyors for the survey of islands or other designated parcels.

Information contained in the contracts includes name of the contracting surveyor; date the contract was issued; date the survey was to be completed; description of the survey work to be done, citing range and township and the type of lines to be run; rate of pay; and estimated cost of the survey. Beginning in 1896, the contract and surveyor's bond were combined on a single printed sheet. The bond lists the person or company acting as surety for the deputy surveyor. Some contracts are accompanied by additional documents relating to the execution of the survey, which may include petitions from settlers to the surveyor general requesting that a particular tract be surveyed, correspondence between deputy surveyors and the surveyor general, supplemental instructions, oath of the deputy surveyor, and diagrams of the area to be surveyed.

The record of contracts and special instructions cites the name of the deputy surveyor, date the contract or instructions were issued, tract to be surveyed, date the survey notes were returned to the surveyor general's office, and dates the plats and transcripts were transmitted to the GLO and the local land office.

Arrangement: Each subseries is chronological by date contract or special instructions issued.

Related Records: The type of supplementary material that accompanies some of the contracts also exists for most of the other contracts but is dispersed in several different series: **Petitions for Surveys; Letters Sent; Letters Received**; and **Surveyors' Accounts.**

Descriptive Lists of Survey Posts, 1849-1907. 6.0 c.f. (4 oversize boxes)
Compiled lists describing survey reference points and locations of section, quarter section, and meander posts for each township in Minnesota. They also include comments on the topography, soil quality,

and plant cover of each section. The lists were compiled by the surveyor general's office from information in the deputy surveyors' field notes and, in effect, are an abstract of the field notes. Some of the lists are dated and signed by the surveyor general. Lists for several townships are missing.

Arrangement: By county, thereunder by range and township. Records for a particular township may be filed under more than one county or, more often, under the county in which the largest part of the township is located.

Field Notes: Township Exterior and Subdivision Survey Lines, 1848-1907. 30.0 c.f. (30 boxes)

Handwritten copies of the notebooks kept by deputy surveyors as they laid out the exterior and subdivision lines of each township, recording survey reference points and the location of section, quarter section, and meander posts. They also include plat drawings and comments on the topography, soil quality, plant cover, and other natural features of each township. The field notes for each township also give the names of the deputy surveyor and his assistants, dates the survey was begun and completed, affidavits attesting to the accuracy of the survey, and the surveyor general's certification of the accuracy of the copied notes.

These copies were made by the surveyor general's office. Some were made immediately after completion of the survey; others were done much later. Several are identified as copies of copies. The series includes both bound volumes containing field notes for several townships and interfiled folders of unbound notes for single townships.

This is not a complete set of survey field notes. Notes for some townships are missing from volumes. The original notebooks are (1985) in the custody of the Minnesota secretary of state's office.

Arrangement: By principal meridian, then range, then township. Bound volumes containing several ranges sometimes slightly disrupt this sequence.

Related Records: **Descriptive Lists of Survey Posts; Township Survey Plats; Field Notes of Survey Examiners.**

Field Notes of Survey Examiners, 1857-1897. 1.0 c.f. (1 box)

Field notes of deputy surveyors commissioned by the surveyor general to examine the accuracy and completeness of surveys of township and subdivision lines, guide meridians and standard parallels, and boundaries of Indian reservations.

The field notes consist of 33 "pocket diaries" (1854-1888) and twelve folders of folios (1889-1897). Field notes include the name of the examining surveyor, the survey to be examined, and the name of the original surveyor and date of his contract. They report on the accuracy of location and quality of construction of survey posts, condition of the blazed survey lines, accuracy of the original survey notes and plats, and any corrections the examiner made in the original survey. Some field notes are accompanied by, or incorporate, a daily journal which may include an account of the trip to and from the survey site, a record of expenses, comments on the weather, and daily notes on the progress of the examination.

Field notes for 1854-1857 are copies of originals obtained from the surveyor general's office at Dubuque, Iowa. These include several volumes of field notes of original surveys of township lines, guide meridians, and standard parallels.

Also included are a journal (log) of survey examinations by Edward Atwater (1857-1858) and an account of expenditures by examiner George B. Wright (1862).

Arrangement: Chronological, by date examination completed.

Related Records: **Field Notes; Descriptive Lists of Survey Posts; Township Survey Plats.**

Letters Received, 1857-1907. 7.3 c.f. (7 boxes and 9 folders)

Letters received by the surveyor general's office in St. Paul relating to all aspects of the survey of public lands in Minnesota. The letters are from three main types of correspondents: U.S. General Land Office (GLO) personnel, deputy surveyors, and private citizens and corporations.

GLO letters predominate. They deal with annual appropriations for survey work in Minnesota; instructions to the surveyor general and deputy surveyors; requests and authorizations for surveys of particular parcels; surveys of Indian reservations and railroad lands; hiring and payment of deputy surveyors and office staff; approval or rejection of completed surveys; illegal cutting of timber on public lands; contested surveys and land claims; and much routine office correspondence such as acknowledgments of reports transmitted and accounts paid.

Deputy surveyors' letters, often from field camps, report progress of survey work; ask the surveyor general for instructions, extensions of contractual deadlines, or payment on contracts; and request information on employment and the awarding of contracts.

Letters from the public and corporations consist of petitions to have particular parcels surveyed; allegations of inaccuracies in completed surveys; inquiries to the surveyor general on survey progress, preemption rights, and the availability of land; and applications for employment.

Other correspondents include registers and receivers of local land offices, county surveyors, private surveyors, and land agents.

Arrangement: Primarily chronological (50 vols.); also includes loose papers (3 folders) and subject files (6 folders and 1 vol.). There may be additional letters relating to the subject files in the bound volumes.

Related Records: **Petitions for Surveys; Accounting Records.** Also, **U.S. General Land Office: Calendar of General Land Office Letters** (page 64) includes citations to letters sent to and received from surveyors general.

Letters Sent, 1854-1908. 4.0 c.f. (4 boxes)

Handwritten and letterpress copies of outgoing letters of the surveyor general's offices in Detroit (1854-1857) and St. Paul (1857-1908) relating to the survey of public lands in Minnesota and parts of Michigan. Recipients fall into three major categories: U.S. General Land Office (GLO) personnel, deputy surveyors, and the general public.

Letters and reports to the GLO form the largest part of the series and include annual reports on the progress of the survey; quarterly and annual accounts; transmissions of deputy surveyors' field notes and plats to the GLO for approval; pay vouchers for surveyors and office staff; responses to inquiries from the GLO concerning allegations of inaccurate surveys, contested land claims, and illegal timber cutting; reports and inquiries on surveying of Indian reservations and railroad lands; requests for authorization to survey particular parcels in response to petitions from the public; and much routine office correspondence.

Letters to the deputy surveyors concern the awarding of contracts; instructions for conduct of surveys; payment on contracts; extension of contractual deadlines; and allegations of inaccurate or improperly conducted surveys.

Letters to the general public include responses to petitions for the survey of particular parcels; to inquiries about the progress of the survey, preemption rights, and the availability of land; to allegations of inaccurate surveys and contested land claims; and to requests for employment.

Other correspondents include registers and receivers of local land offices, county surveyors, private surveyors, and land agents.

Arrangement: Chronological within three subseries: Vols. J-Q, 1854-1889 (handwritten); Vols. 1-19, 1884-1908 (letterpress); and Chief Clerk, 1853-1869.

Finding Aids: Most volumes are indexed by recipient.

Related Records: **U.S. General Land Office: Calendar of General Land Office Letters** (page 64) includes citations to letters sent to and received from surveyors general.

Miscellaneous Maps and Lists, undated and 1850-1914. 0.4 c.f. (7 folders)

Plat maps and sketches showing progress of the Minnesota land survey, Indian reservation boundaries, part of the Fort Ripley and Red River Road, plats available from Jewett and Son, a list of townships surveyed, and hand-drawn or blueprint plats of various towns and cities. Although they were found with the records of the U.S. Surveyor General, the actual provenance of many of the plats is unknown.

Miscellaneous Records, 1857-1907. 0.7 c.f. (13 vols. and 7 folders)

Miscellaneous reports, inventories, and manuals produced or used by the surveyor general's office. They include annual reports to the General Land Office (1896-1906), office inventories, reports to GLO inspectors, survey instructions, almanacs, a list of original land entries for parts of St. Paul, various office work records, and miscellany.

Arrangement: By record type, thereunder chronological.

Related Records: Annual reports prior to 1896 are filed in **Letters Sent.**

Petitions for Surveys, undated and 1858-1907. 1.0 c.f. (1 box)

Petitions and letters received by the surveyor general's office requesting that particular townships or islands be surveyed.

The petitions for survey of townships list the township and range number, names of at least three settlers in the township (General Land Office policy required that there be at least three bona fide settlers before a petition would be considered), and a statement by the settlers as to the type and value of any improvements they had made and the length of time they had resided in the township. Some petitions include other descriptive information about the township and the extent of settlement. Most are signed by the petitioners and witnesses. The petitions for surveys of islands include descriptions of the island's location and approximate size, and usually contain affidavits listing the owners of adjacent shore property and stating the occupancy history of the island.

The petitions are in the form of personal letters, standardized forms, and letters from lawyers and land agents. Many petitions from the earlier years are included in the bound volumes of **Letters Received.**

Arrangement: Chronological.

Related Records: **Letters Received; Contracts for Surveys.**

Plats of Township Boundaries, 1857-1907. 0.75 c.f. (294 items)

Plats of various township boundaries drawn by the surveyor general's office from deputy surveyors' field notes. The surveyor general's office sometimes contracted for surveys of only the exterior lines of townships on designated range and township lines. These townships were subdivided under later contracts for survey. The boundary plats show survey reference points, bearings, and distances, and indicate the type of plant cover along the township boundaries.

Arrangement: A list of the township boundary plats in the order in which they are filed accompanies the records.

Related Records: **Township Survey Plats; Field Notes.**

Surveyors' Accounts, 1880-1884, 1896-1906. 0.4 c.f. (8 folders)

Accounts of deputy surveyors for work done under contracts or special instructions from the surveyor general. Accounts include the following information: name of the deputy surveyor, date the contract or special instructions were issued, description of the area surveyed, type of survey (base lines, township lines, etc.), proportions to be paid at the high and low rates depending on difficulty of the work, total cost of survey, surveyor general's approval of the accounts, and date approved.

Arrangement: Chronological by date the contract or special instructions were issued.

Related Records: **Contracts for Surveys**, **Letters Sent**, and **Letters Received** contain correspondence relating to payment of deputy surveyors and disputes over the cost of survey work.

Swamp Land Lists, 1863-1907. 9.0 c.f. (6 oversize boxes)

Lists of "swamp and overflowed" land compiled by the U.S. Surveyor General from the field notes of the deputy surveyors. All public land designated "swamp and overflowed" was granted to the state of Minnesota by congressional acts of September 28, 1850, and March 12, 1860.

As the general survey of public land was completed, the surveyor general determined which of the surveyed land fell within the definition of the swamp land grant. Copies of the lists were forwarded to the local land offices of the General Land Office (GLO) where the designated tracts were checked against the GLO records for prior claims or reservations. Copies were also sent to the State Land Office for use in preparing swamp land selection lists. This series is a merged file of records from the GLO, State Land Office, and U.S. Surveyor General. There are duplicate copies of many lists but for some only one copy exists.

The swamp land lists are arranged by GLO land district and thereunder by date filed by the surveyor general. They contain the following information: land district in which the designated land was located; legal description of the swamp and overflowed tracts, citing the range, township, section, and fractional section; name of river, watercourse, or other cause that rendered the tract "swamp and overflowed" within the meaning of the grant; statement of the grounds for the surveyor general's designation of the listed tracts as swamp and overflowed; and date the surveyor general submitted the lists to the local land office. Some lists include annotations made by the register and receiver of the local land office indicating disposition of the land.

Related Records: **State Land Office: Swamp Land Selection Lists** (page 24).

Timber Agent Accounts and Correspondence, 1861-1877. 0.2 c.f. (2 folders and 1 vol.)

Records of the surveyor general acting as timber agent, charged with protecting the federal government's interest in timber on public and reserved lands.

Correspondence with the General Land Office, U.S. marshals, logging companies, private parties, and log scalers relates to alleged illegal cutting of government timber, issuing of logging permits, payment for logs cut on government land, and the appointment of scalers. Accounts include itemized records of expenditures by the timber agent and his deputies, vouchers, and receipts for sale of stumpage. A stumpage sale record (1874-1877, 1 vol.) cites the township on which timber was cut, the footage cut, log mark, by whom cut, and to whom sold.

Related Records: Accounts of expenditures for 1862-1877 are located in the volume titled "Quarterly Accounts" in the series **Accounting Records.**

Township Survey Plats (Official Set), 1847-1976 (bulk 1847-1870s). 2540 microfiche.

Microfiche reproductions of the plat drawings of Minnesota townships made by the U.S. surveyor general's office in St. Paul from the field notes of deputy surveyors.

Plats for each township show section and subdivision markers; acreage of some subdivisions; rivers, lakes, swamps, major land elevations, and other natural features; location and identification of any settlements or settlers' claims established prior to the completion of the survey; and any roads or railroads in existence at the time of the survey. Some plats include names of streams and lakes, notes on topography and vegetation, meander notes, and related data.

The plats also list the total acreage of the township; name of the surveyor(s); date of contract or special instructions under which the township was surveyed; date the survey was completed; and date the plats were approved by the surveyor general. Some townships that are divided by a major watercourse have two plats, one for each bank. There are additional plats for some townships in which subsequent surveys were made to correct or reestablish section or subdivision markers, or for surveys of islands that were not included in the original government survey.

Filmed with each plat is a certificate of authenticity signed by the Minnesota secretary of state.

Originals of the plats are (1985) in the Minnesota secretary of state's office.

Arrangement: By principal meridian, then range, then township; one township per fiche. Each microfiche has an alphanumeric identification symbol that reflects the initial filming order of the plats.

Finding Aids: A computer-generated index, although not needed to locate the plat for a given township, contains summary data on each plat. See **Township Survey Plats: Index.**

Township Survey Plats (Supplemental Set), ca.1857-ca.1907. 3.0 c.f. (2 oversize boxes)

Plat drawings of Minnesota townships made by the surveyor general's office from deputy surveyors' field notes.

Plats for each township show section and subdivision markers; lakes, rivers, swamps, and other natural features; location and identification of any settlers' claims established prior to completion of the survey; roads and railroads in existence at the time of the survey; and boundaries of any Indian reservations crossing the township.

The surveyor general's office produced several copies of each plat. This set (some of which may in fact be the original drawings of the deputy surveyors) is not complete. It includes only a few plats for townships surveyed under the Dubuque surveyor general's office prior to 1857, and plats for various other townships are missing. The most complete set of plats is held by the Minnesota secretary of state. This official set is available on microfiche, listed as **Township Survey Plats (Official Set).**

Arrangement: Primarily by range and township; one folder of miscellaneous plats.

Related Records: **Field Notes: Township Exterior and Subdivision Survey Lines; Descriptive Lists of Survey Posts.**

Township Survey Plats: Index, ca.1984. 2 microfiche.

Computer-generated index to the official set of Minnesota township plats filed in the Minnesota secretary of state's office. Each entry gives township and range, sections surveyed, month and year of survey, surveyor's code number, lines surveyed, comments, plat type (original, resurvey, or copy), and file reference (microfiche number). There may be several index entries for a single township or range if portions were surveyed, resurveyed, or annotated at different times.

The index was generated from a file residing at the University of Minnesota Computer Center.

Arrangement: One fiche for the 4th prime meridian and one for the 5th. Each is arranged by township number, then range number, within groups of ranges: 4th P.M. ranges 12-21, 21-32; 5th P.M. ranges 3-28, 28-34, 35-41, 41-51.

Related Records: This series is an index to **Township Survey Plats (Official Set).**

U.S. GENERAL LAND OFFICE

The records of the U.S. General Land Office document the initial transfer of title to public land in Minnesota from the federal government to private individuals, corporations, and the state of Minnesota. The General Land Office (GLO) records in the State Archives comprise about 330 cubic feet of registers of entries, tract books, correspondence, and administrative records covering the period from 1848 to 1930. The GLO records are the basis of all land titles in Minnesota and are valuable for a wide variety of historical research.

The General Land Office was established as a bureau within the Treasury Department by an act of Congress of April 25, 1812, and was responsible for managing the disposition of the federal domain. Prior to this act three departments had been involved in the disposition of government land. The secretary of the treasury supervised the sale of land, the secretary of war was responsible for managing military bounty land warrants, and the secretary of state countersigned all patents. The commissioner of the GLO assumed responsibility for all aspects of the disposition of the public domain. The Office of Surveyor General was added to the GLO's jurisdiction in 1836, but the survey and land disposition functions operated independently of each other. In 1849 the GLO was made part of the newly established Department of the Interior.

The transfer of the General Land Office from the Treasury Department to the Interior Department in some ways reflected the two major attitudes on the proper role of the public domain in federal policy, each of which carried implications for the organization and operations of the GLO. On the one hand were those who viewed the public domain primarily as a source of revenue, a policy which critics charged favored the accumulation of large, speculative holdings and slowed settlement of the West. The opposing group regarded the raising of revenue as a secondary, though not insignificant, consideration. They believed the principal aim of federal policy should be getting land into the possession of actual settlers, a position eventually embodied in the "free land" provisions of the Homestead Act of 1862. The contradictions between these attitudes were never fully resolved, prompting one scholar to describe the federal land policy as "an incongruous system."[2]

By the time the first land in what would become Minnesota was opened for entry in 1848, the GLO had developed standardized administrative structures and procedures that applied to all the public land states.

The earliest sales of federal land were conducted by public auction and held in the national capital and larger cities of the East. In response to western wishes that land sales be held near the tracts being sold,

---

2. Paul Wallace Gates, History of Public Land Law Development, Chapter XVI (Washington, D.C., 1968), pp. 435-462.

Congress in 1800 established four land districts in Ohio, each with a land office to conduct land sales. The land district became the basic administrative unit of the GLO. The GLO quickly adopted the policy that land could be entered only at the land office of the land district in which it was situated. As westward settlement proceeded, Congress authorized the creation of new land districts. The creating legislation specified the inclusive bounds of the district and sometimes named the district and designated the site of the first land office. If the land office site was not specified, the president was empowered to determine its location. The president could also order the transfer of a land office to a more convenient location within the district. By law, land offices were to be closed and land districts consolidated when less than 100,000 acres of land in the district remained open for entry.

Each land office was staffed by two principal officers, a register and a receiver, assisted by several clerks and transcribers. The register and receiver were appointed by the president and the positions became important parts of the patronage system.

The register was responsible for recording each entry in the appropriate register of entries and noting each parcel entered in the tract books and township plats. Separate registers were kept for each of the various categories of land entries. The receiver of the land office accepted money in payment for land purchases and for fees and commissions due on other types of entries. The receiver kept a "register of receipts" for each type of entry, paralleling the information recorded in the registers of entries. This gave the land office two complete records of entries, each being a full check on the other. Copies of both the registers of entries and the registers of receipts were forwarded to the GLO each month so that, in effect, a full record of entries was maintained both in the local land office and in the GLO offices in Washington, D.C.

The register and receiver were also responsible for maintaining correspondence files and a variety of accounts and administrative records. In addition, the register and receiver acted as a quasi-judicial body in ruling on contested cases in which two or more parties sought to enter the same parcel or in which the validity of an entry was challenged. In such cases the register and receiver conducted hearings at which the claimants presented testimony and affidavits in support of their entries. On the basis of the evidence presented and the records of the land office, the register and receiver upheld or denied the contested entry. If they differed in their opinions on a case it was forwarded to the commissioner of the GLO for decision. Contest decisions of the register and receiver could be appealed to the commissioner and ultimately to the secretary of the interior.

The principal mechanisms through which land was conveyed from the federal government were public auctions, private cash purchases, warrant and scrip entries, homestead and timber culture entries, and grants to the states and to railroads. Critical to the operation of these mechanisms were the practice of preemption and the distinction between "offered" and "unoffered" land.

The term "unoffered land" denoted public land, both surveyed and unsurveyed, that had not been offered for sale at public auction. "Offered land" was land that had been offered for sale at auction and was subject to private entry. By law, all land that had been surveyed and was to be opened for entry had first to be offered for sale at public auction. The date of the auction was set by a presidential proclamation listing the tracts to be sold. Each forty acre parcel was "cried" by an auctioneer and sold to the highest bidder with a minimum price of $1.25 per acre. The sale continued until all of the listed tracts had been offered for bid. Any land for which a minimum bid was not received was then subject to private entry.

Prior to 1841 it was illegal to take up residence on unoffered land. A series of laws had been passed to prevent illegal settling on public land and an act of 1807 provided for the forced removal of "squatters" or preemptors. In fact, these laws proved ineffective as settlers continued to move onto and improve unoffered and even unsurveyed land.

When this preempted land was to be offered for sale at auction, the settlers faced the prospect of losing their claims to the highest bidders. The preemptors often organized "claim clubs" that sought to delay the scheduling of sales or, when sales were held, attempted to prevent bidding on preempted claims. The settlers also petitioned Congress for legislation recognizing their claims and permitting them to enter the land at the minimum price. Several retrospective preemption acts were passed but each was applicable only for a certain area and for a short duration. It was not until 1841 that a general, prospective preemption law was enacted. This act recognized the claims of settlers on surveyed but unoffered land. An act of 1854 extended preemption rights to settlers on unsurveyed land in Minnesota. By filing a declaratory statement with the local land office, the preemptor could protect his claim and later purchase it at the minimum price.

With the exception of several sales of prime timber land, relatively few acres of land were sold by auction in Minnesota, and very few of these brought more than the minimum price. In part this was due to the activities of the claim clubs and collusion between potential bidders, but it also reflected a general reluctance to risk bidding up the price of a parcel that could later be purchased at $1.25 per acre.

Private cash purchases, scrip and warrant entries, and homestead and timber culture entries were discrete, private transactions by an individual, as opposed to the public nature of the auctions. The terms "to enter," "to locate," or "to file on" were used to denote the process of acquiring government land by "private entry." In GLO parlance, the person locating land was an "entryman."

The procedures for entering land by cash purchase, scrip, or warrant were similar. If the entryman had not preselected the parcel he wished to enter, he could examine the plat maps and tract books at the local land office to determine what land was available for entry. After deciding which parcel he wanted to enter, the entryman filed an application to enter the land with the register of the land office. The register checked the plats and tract books to ensure that the parcel was not subject to any prior entries. The entryman then proceeded to the receiver and paid the purchase price, in cash, scrip, or warrant, as well as any fees and commissions due on the entry. The receiver issued a receipt and recorded the transaction in the register of receipts. The receipt was then presented to the register, who recorded the entry in the tract books, plats, and appropriate register of entries. The entryman was issued a certificate of purchase that established his claim to the parcel pending the issuance of a patent by the GLO in Washington, D.C. There was often a three- to six-month delay between the date of entry and the issuance of a patent.

Warrants and scrip were a form of government paper entitling the bearer to enter a specified amount of land. The warrants had been issued as bonuses for service in the military, and the various types of scrip were given either in lieu of an actual grant of land or as an indemnity to certain dispossessed claimants. The warrants and scrip were issued in various denominations, usually 40, 80, or 160 acres. Warrants could be used only to locate offered land while some types of scrip could be used to enter unoffered and unsurveyed land. Most warrants and script were assignable, and a brisk business in land paper developed. Every land office town had its dealers in warrants and scrip. The warrants and scrip had a nominal value of $1.25 per acre but were discounted by brokers at prices ranging from $.62 to $1.15 per acre. Many large scale speculators and land dealers made extensive use of warrants and scrip in acquiring their holdings.

Homestead and timber culture entries represented the culmination of the movement for free public land. The Homestead Act of 1862 permitted homesteaders to obtain title to up to 160 acres of land by living on and improving a claim for five years. The Timber Culture Act of 1873 allowed individuals to acquire an additional 160 acres by planting a specified portion to trees. Homestead and timber culture entries could be made on offered land and on surveyed unoffered land.

An individual seeking to acquire land under the Homestead Act first filed an application or "declaratory statement" with the local land office. If the selected parcel was available for entry, a certificate of entry was issued which established the entryman's claim to the parcel. The homesteader was then required to live on and improve the land for five years. After this time the homesteader "proved up" his claim by presenting the local land office with a "final proof" of his compliance with the Homestead Act. If the land office accepted the final proof, a "final certificate" was issued. The final certificate was then turned in to the General Land Office and a patent was issued formally transferring title to the homesteader. The procedure for making timber culture entries was essentially similar except that residence on the tract was not required.

The land grants to the state were conveyed either by direct legislative enactment or by a sequence of selection and approved lists. The Minnesota statehood act (1857) transferred title to sections 16 and

36 of each township to the state for school purposes. For other categories of trust fund land the state chose the tracts it wished to receive by filing selection lists with the local land offices. The selection lists were examined by the registers and receivers and the commissioner of the GLO for conflicting claims, and if none existed the secretary of the interior approved the selected land for patenting to the state.

The federal government granted land to several railroads to aid in the construction of their lines in Minnesota. The state of Minnesota served as a conduit in the administration of these grants. The granted lands were patented to Minnesota and the state then deeded the land to the railroad as prescribed by the terms of the grant. Records of grant lands selected by these railroads were also maintained by the GLO.

The General Land Office records have been organized by land district and thereunder by record series. The only exceptions to this are several series, including original entry tract books and records of state and railroad land grants, that have been arranged by record series without regard to land district. There were eleven land districts in Minnesota: Alexandria, Cass Lake, Crookston, Duluth, Minneapolis, Ojibway (no records exist for this district), Red Wing, Root River, St. Cloud, Stillwater, and Winona. District names are taken from the act establishing the district or from the district's most significant land office. The boundaries of some districts changed considerably over the years as new districts were carved out of old, land was transferred from one district to another, and districts were closed and consolidated.

When the land office of a district was transferred to a new location the records were simply carried forward. As land districts were closed their records were transferred to the land office of the successor district. By 1908 only the Cass Lake, Crookston, and Duluth land districts remained in existence. The records of all other districts had been transferred to Duluth. The Crookston and Duluth districts were closed in 1925 and the records were transferred to the Minnesota Historical Society. The society also acquired the records of Cass Lake when that district was closed in 1933.

Many of the GLO records are pre-printed forms that were filled in by the register or receiver. For some series the record form was changed or renamed over the years, or an inappropriate form may have been used, but the informational content remained the same. In such cases, the State Archives has established uniform series titles that may differ from the title on a particular volume spine or page, in order that similar records will have similar series titles in all land districts. In addition, many sets of volumes have been assigned sequential volume numbers, to assist users in locating and identifying them.

There are several broad categories of records found in each land district: registers of entries, abstracts, record books of various types, and correspondence. The registers of entries are the principal record of land entered in each district. Separate registers were kept for each type of entry, and each type of register is treated as a distinct record series. The abstracts are records of transactions preliminary to an entry, such as the abstracts of declaratory statements. Series titled "Record of . . ." are in-office administrative records such as the Record of Patents Delivered or Record of Letters Received. There are several series of correspondence in each district including Letters Received, Register's Letters Sent, and Receiver's Letters Sent.

The completeness of the records varies from district to district. The Stillwater district appears to be missing several entire series as well as portions of others. The Crookston records are by far the most complete. Some types of records and accounts, although fragmentary and/or extant for only one or two land districts, were retained to demonstrate the full scope of the land system operations. Presumably, the records that are missing from the Historical Society's General Land Office records can be found in the GLO records in the National Archives (Record Group 49, Bureau of Land Management; and Record Group 48, Interior Department, Records of the Lands and Railroads Division).

The several series of aggregate GLO records that cross district lines are described on the next three pages. They are followed by capsule histories of the ten land districts for which records are extant, each accompanied by a list of the record series found in the State Archives for that district. Following the district histories are alphabetically arranged descriptions of each discrete type of record, including in many instances summaries of the law or process that generated the record, with each description being followed by a list of the land districts for which that record is present.

U.S. GENERAL LAND OFFICE
GENERAL RECORDS

Calendar of General Land Office Letters, 1794-1926. 9.1 c.f. (3" x 5" cards)

Calendars of letters sent and received by the commissioner of the General Land Office relating to the survey and sale of public land in Minnesota and the "Old Northwest Territory" generally.

This calendar of GLO letters is a portion of the "Mereness Calendar" of federal records relating to the states of the "Old Northwest Territory." The Mereness calendar was created between 1909 and 1937 under the auspices of the Conference of State Historical Agencies of the Upper Mississippi Valley. This calendar represents that portion of the Mereness calendar of GLO correspondence that relates to Minnesota in a specific or general way.

Each card calendars one letter and includes the following information: date of letter, person by whom sent, person to whom sent, summary of subject of letter, and citations to location of the letter in the records of the GLO giving the GLO record series, volume, and page number. Each card also includes a "Mereness card number" and an alphabetic code indicating the state(s) to which the letter is relevant (a-Indiana, b-Michigan, c-Wisconsin, d-Illinois, e-Iowa, f-Minnesota).

The calendar of GLO letters is divided into several subseries based on the arrangement of the GLO records in Washington, D.C.: letters sent to surveyors general (1831-1901), letters received from surveyors general (1794-1879), miscellaneous letters (1796-1868), townsites (1856-1913), letters to members of congress (1868-1887), abandoned military reservations (1848-1925), miscellaneous letters received (1805-1822), private land claims (1833-1895), swamp land, railroad land, and maps.

Arrangement: Chronological within each subseries.

Related Records: Calendars of several series of Interior Department correspondence relating to public land and railroad grants, 1849-1880 (not described in this guide).

Circular Letters Received, 1855-1908. 0.2 c.f. (4 folders)

An incomplete set of circular letters sent to the registers and receivers of all land offices by the commissioner of the GLO, secretary of the treasury, and comptroller of the treasury department. It was compiled largely from circulars received by the Duluth land district.

The circular letters include announcements of changes in GLO policies and procedures, instructions to registers and receivers, and proclamations announcing land sales, the removal of land offices to new locations, and changes in land district boundaries.

Copies of many of these letters are in the series **Letters Received** for the various land districts. The Letters Received may include additional circular letters not present in this series.

Arrangement: Chronological.

Miscellaneous Maps, undated, 1870-1872, 1913-1925. 0.3 c.f. (4 oversize folders)
Miscellaneous maps and plats from various local land offices, and plats of highway rights of way across Indian land (1913-1925).

Original Entry Tract Books, 1848-ca.1930. 46 rolls microfilm.
Tract books kept by the Minnesota local offices of the General Land Office to provide a consolidated record of the initial transfer of title to federal land from the United States to private parties or to the state of Minnesota. For each parcel of land they give its legal description, acreage, price, name of purchaser or transferree, sale date and certificate number or other disposition data, name of final patentee, date of final patent, and citation to the patent record in the General Land Office records.

Some text is faint or obscure, due to poor condition of the original paper and/or ink. The original records may be made available if data proves to be illegible on the microfilm.

Arrangement: By range and township, but not always consecutively or systematically.

Finding Aids: Tract index at the beginning of roll 1; also available on microfiche as **Original Entry Tract Books: Index.**

Related Records: Letters received and register's and receiver's letters sent for each of Minnesota's several land districts are often cited in the tract books as sources of further documentation on particular land transactions.

Original Entry Tract Books: Index. 3 microfiche.
The index is organized by range and township and cites the volume(s) and page(s) on which entries for land in a particular township appear.

Railroad Selection Lists, 1860-1926. 10.5 c.f. (7 oversize boxes)
The several Minnesota railroads that received congressional grants of public lands to assist in meeting construction expenses were entitled to receive specified amounts of land for each mile of track completed, usually the odd-numbered sections within six miles each side of the line. If any of these lands were already reserved, homesteaded, or otherwise unavailable, the railroad was entitled to select an equivalent amount of public land as indemnity. The Railroad Selection Lists itemize the indemnity lands selected by each railroad and submitted for approval to the General Land Office. They generally, but not always, correspond to the master sets of approved lists and land patents kept by the State Land Office.

The General Land Office, the state auditor, and the railroad each received a copy of every selection list. This series is a merged file of two incomplete sets of records originally located in the General Land Office and the state auditor's office. Occasional relinquishment, homestead indemnity, and railroad approved lists are also present.

Arrangement: By railroad, thereunder by land office and date filed.

Related Records: **Northern Pacific Railway Co. Records: Land Department: Selection Lists** (page 114).

State Trust Fund Land Selection and Approved Lists, 1867-1916. 1.0 c.f. (1 box)

An incomplete set of selection and approved lists for various categories of state trust fund land. The series includes selection lists for indemnity school land and approved lists for indemnity school land, salt spring land, agricultural college land, university land, internal improvement land, and state forestry land. There is also an inventory of state school land.

Under a number of congressional enactments, the federal government granted the state specified amounts of land for designated purposes. To obtain these lands the state filed selection lists in the local land offices, giving the legal description of each tract selected. The selection lists, which established the priority of the state's claim to the tracts selected, were then forwarded to the GLO for approval by the commissioner and the secretary of the interior. The approved lists are derived from the selection lists and itemize those tracts that were approved for patenting to the state.

Arrangement: By type of list, thereunder by land district.

Related Records: The State Land Office records include a more complete set of approved lists.

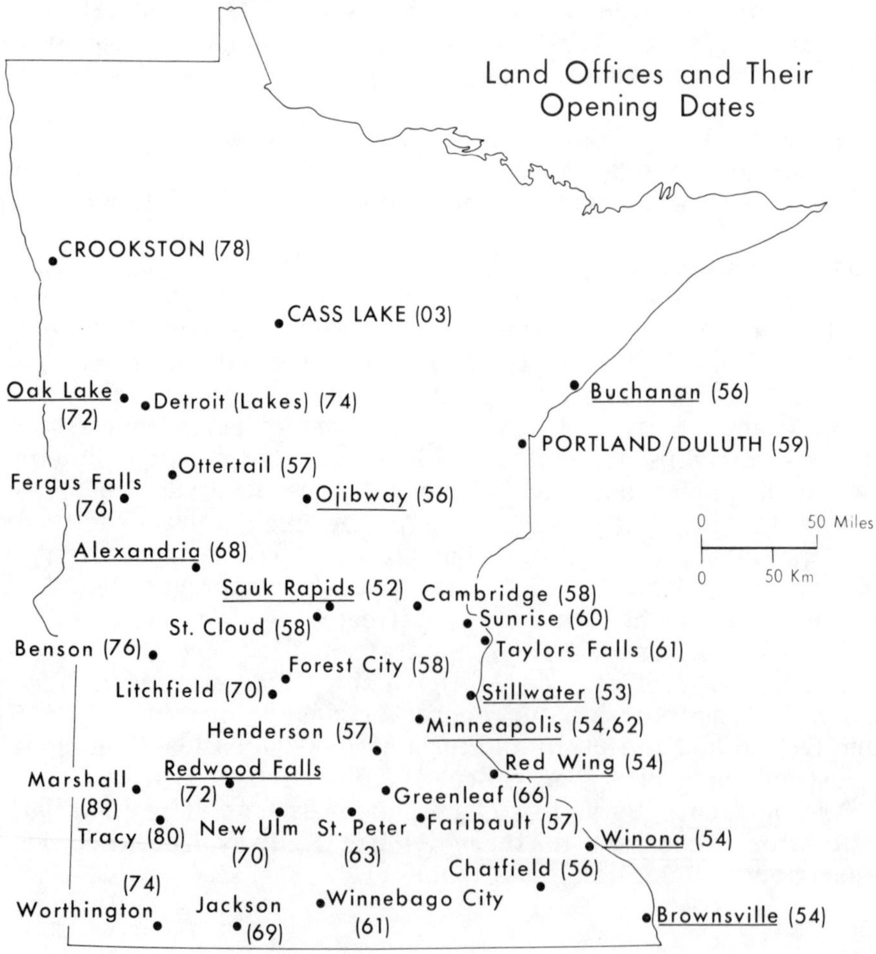

U.S. GENERAL LAND OFFICE LAND DISTRICTS IN MINNESOTA

Alexandria Land District

The Alexandria land district was created out of the western part of the St. Cloud district by an act of Congress of July 25, 1868. The first land office was located in Alexandria and opened for business in November, 1868. The boundaries of the Alexandria land district changed several times. The following description of the boundaries corresponds to the numbered diagrams. All ranges are west of the 5th principal meridian.

1. By the act of 1868 the Alexandria district encompassed townships 121-164 in ranges 36-51.

2. An executive order of August 28, 1871, removed townships 121-124 in ranges 36-49 from the Alexandria district and added them to the Minneapolis district.

3. An act of March 12, 1872, created the Oak Lake (Crookston) land district out of the northern portion of the Alexandria district. The reduced Alexandria district consisted of townships 125-136 in ranges 36-49.

4. On February 28, 1889, the Fergus Falls land office was closed and the Alexandria district was merged into the St. Cloud district.

1

2

3

<u>Land Offices of the Alexandria Land District</u>

Alexandria	Nov. 1868	to	Nov. 24, 1876
Fergus Falls	Dec. 11, 1876	to	Feb. 28, 1889

List of Series:

Abstract of Preemption Declaratory Statements, 1869-1872. Partial vol.
Contest Docket, 1879-1883. 1 vol.
Correspondence: Letters Received from GLO, 1868-1889. 4.0 c.f. (4 boxes)
Correspondence: Receiver's Letters Sent, 1869-1880. 2 vols.
Correspondence: Register's Letters Sent, 1869-1881. 3 vols.
Miscellaneous Records, 1878-1885. 1 folder.
Record of Patents Delivered, 1884-1889. 1 vol.
Register of Certificates to Purchasers, 1869-1889. 1 vol.
Register of Final Homestead Certificates, 1869-1889. 1 vol.
Register of Homestead Entries, 1863-1889. 2 vols.
Register of Military Bounty Land Warrant Entries, 1869-1888. 3 vols.
Register of Timber Culture Entries, 1873-Feb. 1889. Partial vol.

Cass Lake Land District

The Cass Lake land district was created by an executive order of April 1, 1903. The new district consisted of land from the Crookston, Duluth, and St. Cloud land districts. The following description of land included in the Cass Lake district corresponds to the numbered diagrams.

1. Executive order of April 1, 1903:

    a. Townships 146-156 in ranges 30-35 west of the 5th p.m. from Crookston.

    b. Townships 53-64 in ranges 24-27 west of the 4th p.m. from Duluth.

    c. All land north of the Mississippi River in townships 143-152 in ranges 25-29 west of the 5th p.m. from Duluth.

    d. All land south of the Mississippi River in townships 141-145 in ranges 25-29 west of the 5th p.m. from St. Cloud.

    e. Townships 53-55 in ranges 24-27 west of the 4th p.m. from St. Cloud.

2. By executive order of October 3, 1904, townships 153-160 in ranges 25-29 west of the 5th p.m. and townships 65-71 in ranges 24-27 west of the 4th p.m. were added to the Cass Lake land district from Duluth.

1

2

Land Offices of the Cass Lake Land District

Cass Lake	July 1, 1903	to	Jan. 1, 1933

List of Series:

Abstract of Timber and Stone Declaratory Statements, 1903-1908. 1 vol.
Contest Docket, 1903-1908. 1.75 c.f. (5 vols.)
Receiver's Accounts as Disbursing Agent, June 1903-April 1909. 1 vol.
Receiver's Accounts of Transcribing Fees, July 1903-June 1908. 1 vol.
Receiver's Accounts of Unearned Fees, 1903-1908. 2 vols.
Receiver's Monthly Accounts Current, July 1903-June 1908. 1 vol.
Receiver's Monthly Statement of Earned Fees, July 1903-June 1908. 1 vol.
Receiver's Quarterly Accounts Current, 1903-1907. 2 vols.
Record of Application to Make Final Proof, Dec. 1914-July 1926. 1 vol.
Record of Canceled Homestead Entries, 1906-1908. 1 vol.
Record of Daily Cash Receipts and Balances, 1903-1908. 2 vols.
Record of Letters Received, 1903-1909. 3 vols.
Record of Patents Delivered, 1903-1914 (bulk 1904-1908). 2 vols.
Record of Rejected and Suspended Applications and Proofs, 1902-1908. 1 vol.
Register of Certificates to Purchasers, 1903-1908. 2 vols.
Register of Certificates to Purchasers: Chippewa Land, 1903-1908. 2 vols.
Register of Final Homestead Certificates, 1903-1908. 2 vols.
Register of Final Homestead Certificates: Chippewa Land, 1903-1908. 2 vols.
Register of Homestead Entries, 1903-1908. 2 vols.
Register of Homestead Entries: Chippewa Land, 1903-1908. 2 vols.
Register of Military Bounty Land Warrant Entries, 1904-1905. 1 folder.
Register of Surveyor General Scrip Entries, 1904-1905. 1 folder.
Serial Registers, 1908-1925. 2.0 c.f. (7 vols.)

Crookston Land District

The Crookston land district was created out of the northern part of the Alexandria land district by an act of Congress of March 12, 1872. By law the district was called Oak Lake after the site of the first land office, but it came to be generally referred to as the Crookston land district. The boundaries of the district changed several times. The following description of the district boundaries corresponds to the numbered diagrams. All ranges are west of the 5th principal meridian.

1. The Act of March 12, 1872, established the Oak Lake/Crookston district consisting of townships 137-164 in ranges 36-51.

2. By executive order of January 16, 1896, townships 146-168 in ranges 30-35 were added to the Crookston district from St. Cloud.

3. Executive order of April 1, 1903, establishing the Cass Lake land district, removed townships 146-156 in ranges 30-35 from the Crookston district.

1 2 3

Land Offices of the Crookston Land District

Oak Lake	April 1872	to	Oct. 31, 1873
Detroit	ca. Nov. 4, 1873	to	ca. April 12, 1879
Crookston	May 5, 1879	to	April 30, 1925

List of Series:

Abstract of Preemption Declaratory Statements, 1872-1890. 0.9 c.f. (2 vols., 1 partial vol., and 1 folder)

Abstract of Soldiers' Homestead Declaratory Statements, 1872-1893. 1 folder.

Abstract of Timber and Stone Declaratory Statements, 1895-1908. Partial vol.

Contest Affidavits, 1886-1908. 4.5 c.f. (4 boxes and partial box)
Contest Decisions, 1899-1902. 0.5 c.f. (partial box)
Contest Docket, 1880-1913. 5.2 c.f. (15 vols.)
Contest Notices, 1899-1906. 4 folders.
Correspondence: Letters Received from GLO, 1872-1908. 24.0 c.f. (24 boxes)
Correspondence: Miscellaneous Letters Received, 1908-1912. 1.0 c.f. (1 box)
Correspondence: Receiver's Letters Sent, 1876-1908. 1.3 c.f. (11 vols.)
Correspondence: Register's Letters Sent, 1872-1913. 6.0 c.f. (54 vols.)
Correspondence: Register's Miscellaneous Letters Sent, 1897-1908. 9.0 c.f. (69 vols. and 1 folder)
Miscellaneous Records, 1885-1920. 5 folders.
Receiver's Accounts as Disbursing Agent, 1872-1908. 3 vols.
Receiver's Accounts of Transcribing Fees, 1892-1907. 2 vols.
Receiver's Accounts of Unearned Fees, 1895-1908. 0.6 c.f. (5 vols.)
Receiver's Monthly Accounts Current, 1885-1908. 3 vols.
Receiver's Monthly Statement of Earned Fees, 1885-June 1908. 1 vol.
Receiver's Quarterly Accounts Current, 1872-1908. 1.5 c.f. (5 vols.)
Record of Application to Make Final Proof, 1905-June 1908. 1 vol.
Record of Applications for Refunds, 1887-1910. 1 vol.
Record of Canceled Homestead Entries, 1905-1908. 1 vol.
Record of Daily Cash Receipts and Balances, 1885-1908. 2.7 c.f. (11 vols.)
Record of Letters Received, 1896-1910. 1.75 c.f. (6 vols.)
Record of Letters Sent, 1886-1917. 3 vols.
Record of Miscellaneous Applications, 1896-1909. 1.0 c.f. (2 vols. and partial vol.)
Record of Patents Delivered, 1878-1911. 2 vols.
Record of Rejected and Suspended Applications and Proofs, 1896-1908. 1.7 c.f. (4 vols. and partial vol.)
Register of Agricultural College Scrip Entries, June 1872-April 1897. 1 vol.
Register of Certificates to Purchasers, 1872-1908. 1.9 c.f. (6 vols.)
Register of Certificates to Purchasers: Chippewa Land, 1896-1908. 1.25 c.f. (4 vols.)
Register of Final Homestead Certificates, 1873-1908. 2.4 c.f. (6 vols.)
Register of Final Homestead Certificates: Chippewa Land, 1899-1908. 2 vols.
Register of Final Timber Culture Certificates, 1884-1903. 0.7 c.f. (4 vols.)
Register of Homestead Entries, 1872-1908. 3.0 c.f. (8 vols.)
Register of Homestead Entries: Chippewa Land, 1896-1908. 2.0 c.f. (6 vols.)
Register of Indian Allotment Entries: Dawes Act, 1893-1897. 1 vol.
Register of Indian Allotment Entries: Nelson Act, 1901. 1 vol.
Register of Military Bounty Land Warrant Entries, 1873-1888. 1 vol.
Register of Red Lake and Pembina Scrip Entries, 1873-1906. 1 folder.
Register of Sioux Half-Breed Scrip Entries, 1879-1902. 3 leaves.
Register of Supreme Court Scrip Entries, 1879-1894. 17 leaves.
Register of Surveyor General Scrip Entries, 1896-1902. 6 leaves.
Register of Timber Culture Entries, 1873-1891. 0.8 c.f. (4 vols.)

Rejected Applications to Enter Land, 1897-1908. 1.5 c.f. (1 box and partial box)
Rejected Homestead Proofs, 1897-1908. 1.3 c.f. (1 box and partial box)
Serial Registers, 1908-1925. 4.0 c.f. (13 vols.)

Duluth Land District

The Northeastern land district, generally known as the Duluth district, was established by an act of Congress of July 8, 1856. The district's first land office was located in Buchanan and opened for business in September, 1856. The district was originally formed from a part of the Stillwater land district and several tracts were later added to the district. The following description of the boundaries of the Duluth district corresponds to the numbered diagrams.

1. The act of 1856 established the Northeastern (Duluth) land district, consisting of townships 61-64 in ranges 1-6 east of the 4th p.m. and townships 46-70 in ranges 1-18 west of the 4th p.m.

2. An executive order of May 25, 1858, added townships 46-70 in ranges 19-23 west of the 4th p.m. to the Duluth district from the Northwestern district.

3. By executive order of February 27, 1891, all townships north of the Mississippi River in ranges 24-27 west of the 4th p.m. and ranges 25-29 west of the 5th p.m. were added to Duluth from the St. Cloud land district.

4. Executive order of April 1, 1903, creating the Cass Lake land district, removed townships 53-64 in ranges 24-27 west of the 4th p.m. and all land north of the Mississippi River in townships 143-152 in ranges 25-29 west of the 5th p.m. from the Duluth district.

5. An executive order of October 3, 1904, removed additional land from the Duluth district. Townships 65-71 in ranges 24-27 west of the 4th p.m. and townships 153-160 in ranges 25-29 west of the 5th p.m. were transferred to Cass Lake.

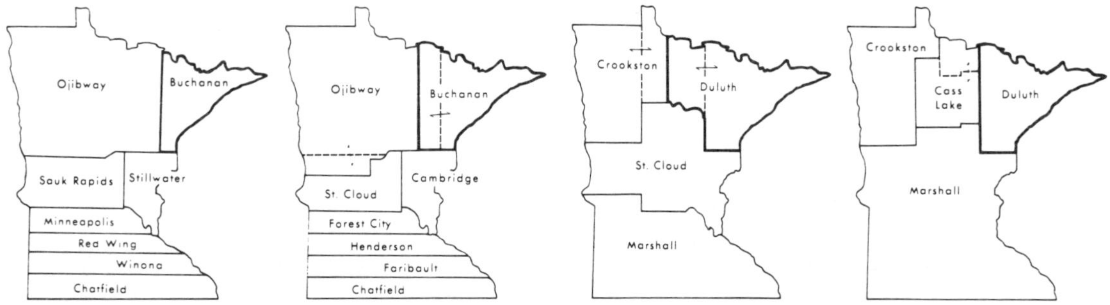

1 2 3 4-5

Land Offices of the Duluth Land District

Buchanan	Sept. 1856	to	ca. May 31, 1859
Portland	ca. June 7, 1859	to	Jan. 15, 1863
Duluth	Jan. 15, 1863	to	April 30, 1925

List of Series:

Abstract of Preemption Declaratory Statements, 1857-1898. 0.75 c.f. (2 vols. and partial vol.)
Abstract of Soldiers' Homestead Declaratory Statements, 1890-1907. 1 vol.
Abstract of Timber and Stone Declaratory Statements, 1892-1908. 3 vols.
Contest Affidavits, 1888-1889. 2 folders.
Contest Decisions, 1904-1911. 0.5 c.f. (3 vols.)
Contest Docket, 1887-1888. 1 vol.
Correspondence, Miscellaneous, 1920-1924. 4 folders.
Correspondence: Letters Received from GLO, 1858-1908. 37.8 c.f. (38 boxes)
Correspondence: Receiver's Letters Sent, 1857-1911. 2.2 c.f. (17 vols.)
Correspondence: Receiver's Miscellaneous Letters Sent, 1890-1907. 0.75 c.f. (6 vols.)
Correspondence: Register's Letters Sent, 1857-1911. 13.0 c.f. (90 vols.)
Correspondence: Register's Miscellaneous Letters Sent, 1900-1911. 3.0 c.f. (19 vols.)
Indian Traders' Applications to Enter Land, 1857-1858. 1 folder.
List of Land Sold: Chippewa Pine Land, 1896-1898. 1 folder.
Notices of Contest Decisions, 1904-1911. 3.0 c.f. (18 vols.)
Receiver's Abstracts of Collections, 1908-1913. 1 vol.
Receiver's Miscellaneous Accounts, 1908-1916. 0.4 c.f. (8 folders)

Record of Patents Delivered, 1861-1908. 1.3 c.f. (4 vols.)
Register of Certificates to Purchasers, 1857-1908. 2.5 c.f. (6 vols.)
Register of Certificates to Purchasers: Chippewa Land, 1896-1908. 1 vol.
Register of Chippewa Half-Breed Scrip Entries, 1858-1880. 1 folder.
Register of Final Homestead Certificates, 1868-1908. 1.5 c.f. (4 vols.)
Register of Final Homestead Certificates: Chippewa Land, 1903-1904. 1 vol.
Register of Forest Reserve Lieu Entries, Sept. 1900-Jan. 1905. 1 vol.
Register of Homestead Entries, 1863-1908. 3.0 c.f. (8 vols.)
Register of Homestead Entries: Chippewa Land, 1896-1908. 2 vols.
Register of Indian Allotment Entries: Dawes Act, 1888-1908. 3 vols.
Register of Indian Allotment Entries: Nelson Act, 1896-1897. 2 folders.
Register of Military Bounty Land Warrant Entries, 1857-1908. 2 vols. and 1 folder.
Register of Sioux Half-Breed Scrip Entries, 1858-1873. 1 folder.
Register of Supreme Court Scrip Entries, July 1874-June 1902. 1 vol. and 1 folder.
Register of Surveyor General Scrip Entries, 1872-1873, 1892-1906. 1 vol. and 1 folder.
Register of Valentine Scrip Entries, 1892-1905. 1 vol.
Serial Registers, 1908-1925. 4.25 c.f. (15 vols. and 4 folders)

Minneapolis Land District

The Minneapolis land district was one of four districts established in the ceded Sioux territory by an act of Congress of April 12, 1854. The district's first land office was located in Minneapolis and opened for business in October, 1854.

The Minneapolis land district, as established by the act of 1854, included townships 116-120 in ranges 20-49 and fractional township 121 in ranges 22-23, all west of the 5th p.m. (fig. 1). By an executive order of August 28, 1871, townships 121-124 in ranges 36-49 were added to the Minneapolis district from the Alexandria district (fig. 2). On February 28, 1889, the Minneapolis land district was merged into the Winona district with land offices first at Tracy and then at Marshall. Entries and other transactions on land in the Minneapolis district dating after March 1, 1889, are recorded in the records of the Winona district.

1

2

Land Offices of the Minneapolis Land District

Minneapolis	ca. Oct. 9, 1854	to	Feb. 27, 1858
Forest City	ca. March 22, 1858	to	Oct. 1, 1862
Minneapolis	Nov. 1, 1862	to	ca. June 15, 1866
Greenleaf	July 3, 1866	to	Dec. 31, 1869
Litchfield	ca. Jan. 1, 1870	to	Sept. 16, 1876
Benson	Oct. 2, 1876	to	Feb. 28, 1889

List of Series:

Abstract of Preemption Declaratory Statements, 1854-1889. 1.0 c.f. (3 vols. and partial vol.)
Abstract of Preemption Declaratory Statements: Sioux Land, 1879-1905 (bulk 1879-1892). 1 vol.
Contest Docket, 1858-1867. Partial vol.
Correspondence: Letters Received from GLO, 1854-1889. 8.0 c.f. (8 boxes)
Correspondence: Receiver's Letters Sent, 1854-1883. 3 vols.
Correspondence: Register's Letters Sent, 1854-1878. 1.5 c.f. (6 vols.)
List of Land Offered for Sale, 1860. 1 vol.
Record of Patents Delivered, July 1884-Feb. 1889. 1 vol.
Register of Agricultural College Scrip Entries, 1863-1873. 1 vol.
Register of Certificates to Purchasers, 1866-1879. 2 vols.
Register of Certificates to Purchasers: Sioux Land, 1869-1902. 0.9 c.f. (5 vols.)
Register of Final Homestead Certificates, 1868-1889. 2 vols.
Register of Homestead Entries, 1863-1889. 1.5 c.f. (6 vols.)
Register of Military Bounty Land Warrant Entries, 1855-1880. 3 folders.
Register of Sioux Half-Breed Scrip Entries, 1857. 1 folder.

Red Wing Land District

The Red Wing land district was one of four districts established in the ceded Sioux territory by an act of Congress of April 12, 1854. The district's first land office was located in Red Wing and opened for business in February, 1855.

The Red Wing land district, as established by the act of 1854, included townships 111-115 in ranges 10-47 west of the 5th p.m. (fig. 1). These bounds remained in effect until April, 1863, when the Red Wing land district was merged into the Winona district (fig. 2). Between April, 1863, and June, 1872, entries and other transactions on land in townships 111-115 were recorded in the records of the Winona land district. The Red Wing land district was re-established in June, 1872, again covering townships 111-115, with a land office at Redwood Falls (fig. 3). On February 28, 1889, the Redwood Falls land office was closed and the Red Wing land district again consolidated into the Winona district with land offices first at Tracy and then at Marshall.

1

2

3

<u>Land Offices of the Red Wing Land District</u>

Red Wing	ca. Feb. 1, 1855	to	ca. June 1, 1857
Henderson	ca. June 1, 1857	to	ca. April 6, 1863

(St. Peter and New Ulm offices of the Winona land district, April 6, 1863-ca. June 1, 1872)

Redwood Falls	ca. June 19, 1872	to	Feb. 28, 1889

<u>List of Series:</u>

Abstract of Preemption Declaratory Statements, 1855-1884. 0.75 c.f. (4 vols.)
Contest Docket, 1872-1880. 1 vol.
Correspondence: Letters Received from GLO, 1855-1863, 1872-1889. 3.25 c.f. (3 boxes and partial box)

Correspondence: Receiver's Letters Sent, 1854-1863, 1872-1889. 1 vol.
Correspondence: Register's Letters Sent, 1855-1889. 1.5 c.f. (4 vols.)
List of Forfeited Homesteads, 1873-1877. Partial vol.
Receiver's Quarterly Accounts Current, Nov. 1855-Feb. 1856. 1 folder.
Record of Patents Delivered, Aug. 1884-Feb. 1889. 1 vol.
Register of Agricultural College Scrip Entries, 1864-1872. 1 folder.
Register of Certificates to Purchasers, 1855-1863, 1872-1889. 0.7 c.f. (5 vols. and 1 folder)
Register of Certificates to Purchasers: Sioux Land, 1872-1889. 1 vol.
Register of Final Homestead Certificates, 1868-1889. 0.75 c.f. (3 vols.)
Register of Homestead Entries, 1862-1889. 1.0 c.f. (3 vols.)
Register of Military Bounty Land Warrant Entries, 1855-1863. 2.0 c.f. (7 vols.)
Register of Sioux Half-Breed Scrip Entries, 1857-1861. 1 vol.
Register of Timber Culture Entries, 1873-1885. 1 vol.

Root River Land District

The Root River land district was one of four districts established in the ceded Sioux territory by an act of Congress of April 12, 1854. The district's first land office was located in Brownsville and opened for business in August, 1854.

The Root River land district included townships 101-105 in ranges 3-47 west of the 5th p.m. The boundaries of the district remained unchanged until March, 1889, when the Root River district was merged into the Winona land district with land offices first at Tracy and then at Marshall. Entries and other transactions on land in townships 101-105 dating after March 1, 1889, are recorded in the records of the Winona land district.

Land Offices of the Root River Land District

Brownsville	Aug. 1854	to	May 30, 1856
Chatfield	June 12, 1856	to	ca. Oct. 16, 1861
Winnebago City	Nov. 14, 1861	to	ca. Aug. 21, 1869
Jackson	Sept. 1, 1869	to	April 10, 1874
Worthington	April 11, 1874	to	ca. Feb. 28, 1889

List of Series:

Abstract of Preemption Declaratory Statements, 1854-1889. 1.3 c.f. (4 vols.)
Abstract of Soldiers' Homestead Declaratory Statements, 1872-1877. 1 folder.
Contest Docket, 1875-1879. 2 vols.
Correspondence: Letters Received from GLO, 1854-1889. 9.0 c.f. (9 boxes)
Correspondence: Receiver's Letters Sent, 1854-1889. 1.2 c.f. (3 vols.)
Correspondence: Register's Letters Sent, 1854-1886. 2.0 c.f. (6 vols.)
List of Suspended Homestead Entries, 1864-1869. 1 folder.
Record of Patents Delivered, 1884-1889. 1 vol.
Register of Agricultural College Scrip Entries, 1863-1875. 1 vol.
Register of Certificates to Purchasers, 1854-1886. 1.2 c.f. (4 vols.)
Register of Final Homestead Certificates, 1868-1889. 2 vols.
Register of Homestead Entries, 1863-1889. 1.8 c.f. (5 vols.)
Register of Military Bounty Land Warrant Entries, 1854-1880. 1.25 c.f. (5 vols.)
Register of Supreme Court Scrip Entries, 1879-1880. 1 vol.
Register of Timber Culture Entries, 1883-Feb. 1889. 1 vol.

St. Cloud Land District

The St. Cloud land district was established by an act of Congress of August 30, 1852. By law the district was named the Sauk River land district, but it came to be commonly known as the St. Cloud land district. The district's first land office was located at Sauk Rapids and opened for business in November, 1852. The boundaries of the St. Cloud district changed several times. At various times the St. Cloud district included lands surveyed under both the 4th and 5th principal meridians. The following boundary descriptions correspond to the numbered diagrams.

1. By the act of 1852 the St. Cloud district included townships 121-168 in ranges 24-51 west of the 5th p.m. and townships 32-47 in ranges 28-33 west of the 4th p.m.

2. By an act of April 12, 1854, townships 32-47 in ranges 28-33 west of the 4th p.m. were removed from St. Cloud and added to the Stillwater land district.

3. An act of July 8, 1856, established the Northwestern and Northeastern land districts. The Northwestern district included that part of the St. Cloud district north of township 133 in ranges 24-51 west of the 5th p.m. and townships 46-71 in ranges 19-27 west of the 4th p.m. This left a reduced St. Cloud district consisting of townships 121-133 in ranges 24-49 west of the 5th p.m.

4. An executive order of May 18, 1858, removed townships 129-133 from St. Cloud to the Northwestern land district.

5. In August, 1863, the Northwestern district was merged into the St. Cloud land district. This created a district consisting of townships 121-168 in ranges 24-51 west of the 5th p.m. and townships 46-71 in ranges 24-27 west of the 4th p.m.

6. An act of July 25, 1868, created the Alexandria district out of the western part of the St. Cloud land district, including townships 121-164 in ranges 36-51 west of the 5th p.m. This left a reduced St. Cloud district composed of townships 121-168 in ranges 24-35 west of the 5th p.m. and townships 46-68 in ranges 24-27 west of the 4th p.m.

7. On February 28, 1889, a reduced Alexandria land district, consisting of townships 125-136 in ranges 36-49, was added to the St. Cloud land district.

8. By executive order of February 27, 1891, all land in the St. Cloud district north of the Mississippi River, including all or parts of townships 54-71 in ranges 24-27 west of the 4th p.m. and townships 143-164 in ranges 25-29 west of the 5th p.m. was removed from St. Cloud and added to the Duluth land district.

9. On January 1, 1894, the Stillwater land district, consisting of townships 26-45 in ranges 15-33 west of the 4th p.m., was merged into the St. Cloud land district.

10. An executive order of January 16, 1896, removed townships 146-168 in ranges 30-35 from the St. Cloud to the Crookston land district.

11. By executive order of April 1, 1903, townships 141-145 in ranges 25-29 west of the 5th p.m. and townships 53-55 in ranges 24-27 west of the 4th p.m. were removed from St. Cloud and added to the new Cass Lake land district.

12. On July 1, 1903, the Winona land district was consolidated with the St. Cloud district.

13. December 16, 1906, the St. Cloud land office was closed and the district merged with Duluth.

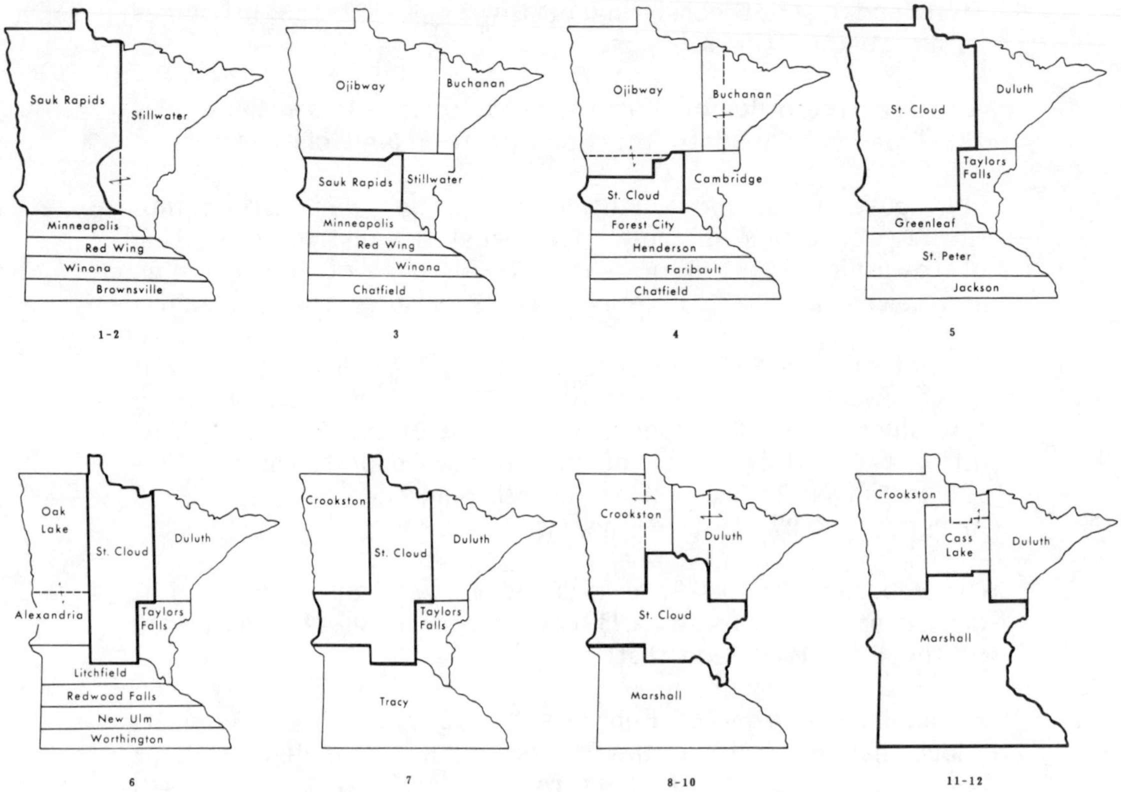

Land Offices of the St. Cloud Land District

Sauk Rapids	Nov. 1852	to	ca. April 15, 1858
St. Cloud	April 29, 1858	to	Dec. 16, 1906

List of Series:

Abstract of Preemption Declaratory Statements, 1853-1905. 2 vols.
Contest Docket, 1880-1888. 1 vol.
Correspondence: Letters Received from GLO, 1853-1906. 25.0 c.f. (25 boxes)
Correspondence: Receiver's Letters Sent, 1853-1879. 2 vols.
Correspondence: Register's Letters Sent, 1860-1879. 1.3 c.f. (4 vols.)
Lists of Land Offered for Sale, 1860-1883. 0.75 c.f. (11 vols.)
Record of Letters Received, 1901-1904. 1 vol.
Record of Patents Delivered, 1884-1907. 1 vol.
Register of Agricultural College Scrip Entries, April 1864-Nov. 1887. Partial vol.

Register of Certificates to Purchasers, 1853-1906. 1.5 c.f. (4 vols.)
Register of Final Homestead Certificates, 1868-1906. 1.2 c.f. (3 vols.)
Register of Homestead Entries, 1863-1906. 1.75 c.f. (5 vols.)
Register of Indian Allotment Entries: Dawes Act, 1889-1902. 1 vol.
Register of Military Bounty Land Warrant Entries, 1853-1906. 1 vol.
Register of Sioux Half-Breed Scrip Entries, 1859-1860. 1 vol.
Register of Supreme Court Scrip Entries, Aug. 1874-June 1885. Partial vol.
Register of Surveyor General Scrip Entries, 1873-1906. 2 partial vols.
Register of Timber Culture Entries, March 1889-1895. Partial vol.

Stillwater Land District

The Stillwater land district, encompassing all of the land in Minnesota territory east of the Mississippi River, was established by an act of Congress of March 2, 1849. This land had been part of the Chippewa land district created in 1847 and encompassing all of Wisconsin Territory north of a line between townships 22 and 23 and west of the Wisconsin River. The act of 1849 created a new land district in the state of Wisconsin and moved the land office of the Chippewa district from the Falls of the St. Croix to Stillwater (fig. 1). All of the land in the Stillwater land district was subject to the survey based on the 4th principal meridian.

An act of August 30, 1852, removed a small parcel of land east of the Mississippi and west of range 27 (townships 32-47 in ranges 28-33) from Stillwater to the new St. Cloud district. These lands were restored to the Stillwater land district by an act of April 12, 1854. The Stillwater district was reduced in size by an act of July 8, 1856, establishing the Northeastern (Duluth) land district north of the line between townships 45 and 46. Between July, 1856, and December, 1893, the Stillwater district encompassed townships 26-45 in ranges 15-33 in the territory and state of Minnesota (fig. 2). On January 1, 1894, the Stillwater land district was merged into the St. Cloud district.

1

2

Land Offices of the Stillwater Land District

Falls of the St. Croix	July 1848	to	Sept. 1849
Stillwater	ca. Oct. 9, 1849	to	Nov. 15, 1858
Cambridge	Dec. 15, 1858	to	ca. May 19, 1860
Sunrise City	ca. July 25, 1860	to	ca. Sept. 30, 1861
Taylors Falls	Oct. 1, 1861	to	ca. Dec. 30, 1893

List of Series:

Abstract of Preemption Declaratory Statements, 1882-1891. 1 vol.
Contest Docket, 1883-1893. 1 vol.
Correspondence: Letters Received from GLO, 1848-1893. 4.0 c.f. (4 boxes)
Correspondence: Receiver's Letters Sent, 1848-1893. 2 vols.
Correspondence: Register's Letters Sent, 1848-1893. 1.7 c.f. (5 vols.)
Proof Right to Preemption, 1871. 1 folder.
Record of Patents Delivered, Aug. 1884-Dec. 1893. 1 vol.
Register of Agricultural College Scrip Entries, 1864-1872. 1 vol.
Register of Certificates to Purchasers, 1875-1893. 1 vol.
Register of Final Homestead Certificates, 1868-1893. 2 vols.
Register of Homestead Entries, 1863-1893. 1.25 c.f. (3 vols.)

Winona Land District

The Winona land district was one of four districts established in the ceded Sioux territory by an act of Congress of April 12, 1854. The district's first land office was located in Winona and opened for business in December, 1854. The boundaries of the Winona land district changed several times. The following boundary descriptions correspond to the numbered diagrams. All ranges are west of the 5th principal meridian.

1. Townships 106-110 in ranges 5-47. Established by act of April 12, 1854, and in effect through April, 1863.

2. Townships 106-115 in ranges 5-47. Between April, 1863, and June, 1872, the Red Wing land district was merged into the Winona district.

3. Townships 106-110 in ranges 5-47. The Red Wing district was re-established in June, 1872, and the Winona district reverted to its original bounds.

4. Townships 101-120 in ranges 3-47, fractional townships 121 in ranges 22-23, and townships 121-124 in ranges 36-49. In March, 1889, the Root River, Red Wing, and Minneapolis land

districts were merged into the Winona land district with land offices first at Tracy and then at Marshall. This enlarged Winona district was in operation until June 23, 1903, when the Marshall office was closed and the district consolidated with the St. Cloud land district.

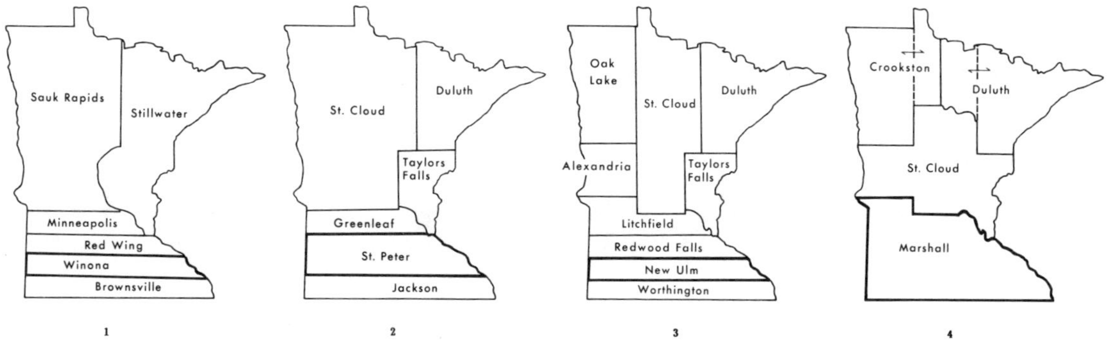

Land Offices of Winona Land District

Winona	Dec. 5, 1854	to	ca. Dec. 31, 1856
Faribault	Jan. 24, 1857	to	Nov. 19, 1858
St. Peter	Dec. 2, 1858	to	ca. Feb. 26, 1870
New Ulm	March 1, 1870	to	ca. April 30, 1880
Tracy	ca. May 2, 1880	to	Feb. 28, 1889
Marshall	March 5, 1889	to	ca. June 23, 1903

List of Series:

Abstract of Preemption Declaratory Statements, 1857-1898. 1.0 c.f. (3 vols.)
Abstract of Soldiers' Homestead Declaratory Statements, 1872-1883. 1 vol.
Contest Docket, 1889-1898. 1 vol.
Correspondence: Letters Received from GLO, 1854-1904. 19.0 c.f. (19 boxes)
Correspondence: Receiver's Letters Sent, 1854-1878. 2 vols.
Correspondence: Register's Letters Sent, 1857-1869. 1 vol. and partial vol.
Homestead Final Proofs, 1870, 1879. 2 folders.
List of Patents for Winnebago Land, 1865-1878. 1 folder.
List of Suspended Preemption Entries, 1855-1861. 1 vol.
Receiver's Estimates of Office Expenditures, 1854-1864. 1 folder.
Record of Patents Delivered, 1884-1903. 1 vol.
Register of Agricultural College Scrip Entries, June 1864-May 1892. 2 vols.
Register of Certificates to Purchasers, 1855-1903. 1.0 c.f. (5 vols.)
Register of Certificates to Purchasers: Sioux Land, 1865-1869. 3 vols.

Register of Certificates to Purchasers: Winnebago Land, 1864-1878. Partial vol.
Register of Chippewa Half-Breed Scrip Entries, 1864. 1 vol.
Register of Final Homestead Certificates, 1868-1903. 3 vols.
Register of Homestead Entries, 1863-1903. 1.5 c.f. (11 vols.)
Register of Military Bounty Land Warrant Entries, 1855-1895. 0.9 c.f. (7 vols.)
Register of Sioux Half-Breed Scrip Entries, 1857-1868. 1 vol.
Register of Supreme Court Scrip Entries, 1859-1880. 1 folder.
Register of Timber Culture Entries, 1886-1897. 1 vol.

DISTRICT LAND OFFICE RECORDS

Abstract of Preemption Declaratory Statements

Abstracts of preemption declaratory statements filed in the various land districts under provisions of the General Preemption Act of 1841.

The preemption act of 1841 recognized the claims of those settlers or "squatters" who had settled on public land before it had been offered for sale. This act enabled the settler to purchase the claim at the minimum price rather than have to bid for it at public auction. The preemptor was required to file a declaratory statement within three months after the local land office had received the survey plat of the township in which the claim was located or within three months of making settlement. The declaratory statement, which gave the date of settlement and detailed the improvements made to the property, was used by the land office to determine the validity of the claimant's preemption and it established the priority of his claim against those of other claimants. When the land office announced that an area of land was to be offered for sale, the preemptor had to pay for his land before the date of the sale or risk losing it to the highest bidder. For land that was open to private entry, the preemptor had to make payment within one year of filing a declaratory statement. In 1854 preemption rights were extended to settlers on unsurveyed land.

The abstract for each declaratory statement includes the following information: statement number, date of settlement, date declaratory statement was filed, name of preemptor, legal description of the tract preempted, and occasional remarks on the eventual disposition of the tract.

Arrangement: Chronological by date statement filed. There are separate sequences for preemptions on "unoffered" lands not yet open for settlement and on "offered" lands which were preempted after being opened for settlement.

Related Records: **Original Entry Tract Books** (page 65). The tract books cite the type and number of the certificate issued on the preempted parcel, and the parcel can then be located in the appropriate register of entries.

Alexandria Land District, 1869-1872. Partial vol.
Crookston Land District, 1872-1890. 0.9 c.f. (2 vols., 1 partial vol., and 1 folder)
Duluth Land District, 1857-1898. 0.75 c.f. (2 vols. and partial vol.)
Minneapolis Land District, 1854-1889. 1.0 c.f. (3 vols. and partial vol.)
Red Wing Land District, 1855-1884. 0.75 c.f. (4 vols.)
Root River Land District, 1854-1889. 1.3 c.f. (4 vols.)
St. Cloud Land District, 1853-1905. 2 vols.
Stillwater Land District, 1882-1891. 1 vol.
Winona Land District, 1857-1898. 1.0 c.f. (3 vols.)

Abstract of Preemption Declaratory Statements: Sioux Land

An incomplete series of abstracts of preemption declaratory statements filed in the Minneapolis land district on land in the former Sioux reservation under provisions of the General Preemption Act of 1841. The series includes statements filed in the Marshall office of the Winona land district after March 1, 1889.

A reservation for the Sioux Indians had been established along the Minnesota River by the Treaty of 1851. In the aftermath of the Dakota War of 1862, the Indians were removed and the land opened for purchase.

Minneapolis Land District, 1879-1905 (bulk 1879-1892). 1 vol.

Abstract of Soldiers' Homestead Declaratory Statements

An abstract of declaratory statements filed by former soldiers seeking to enter additional homestead land under provisions of the Soldiers and Sailors Act of June 8, 1872.

This act, designed to provide a bonus to those who had served in the Civil War, allowed a veteran whose original homestead was 40, 80, or 120 acres to make an additional homestead entry of 120, 80, or 40 acres, respectively. The act also allowed veterans to count their time in service against the residence requirement of the homestead act, thereby permitting them to make final proof after as little as one year's residence on their claims. Originally the act restricted the additional entry to land contiguous to the original homestead. This restriction was lifted by an act of March 3, 1873, which allowed the additional entry to be made on any offered or unoffered land open to homesteading. In addition, the soldiers' rights were made assignable, in effect creating a type of scrip.

The abstract for each declaratory statement includes the following information: statement number, date filed, name of person filing statement, legal description of the parcel applied for, and occasional remarks with citations to letters received from the commissioner of the General Land Office.

Arrangement: Chronological by date statement filed.

Crookston Land District, 1872-1893. 1 folder.
Duluth Land District, 1890-1907. 1 vol.
Root River Land District, 1872-1877. 1 folder.
Winona Land District, 1872-1883. 1 vol.

Abstract of Timber and Stone Declaratory Statements

An abstract of declaratory statements filed under provisions of the Timber and Stone Act of June 2, 1878, as amended August 4, 1892.

The Timber and Stone Act provided that unoffered, unreserved public land valuable chiefly for timber or minerals could be sold to individuals in quantities not to exceed 160 acres at a minimum price of $2.50 per acre. The purchaser had to file a declaratory statement swearing that he did not apply to purchase on speculation and that he intended the entry for his own use. The act of 1878 applied to several western states and territories but was extended to all public land states by the 1892 amendment.

The abstract for each declaratory statement includes the following information: statement number, date filed, name and residence of applicant, legal description of the tract applied for, and occasional annotations citing the certificate number in the **Register of Certificates to Purchasers** or citing letters received from the commissioner of the General Land Office.

Arrangement: Chronological.

Cass Lake Land District, 1903-1908. 1 vol.
Crookston Land District, 1895-1908. Partial vol.
Duluth Land District, 1892-1908. 3 vols.

Contest Affidavits

Affidavits initiating contests against homestead, preemption, and other land entries. Some affidavits are accompanied by other documentation relating to the contest.

The affidavits give the names of the contestant (plaintiff) and the entryman (defendant) in the contest, number and type of the entry being contested, legal description of the tract covered by the contested entry, date the affidavit of contest was filed, grounds of the contest, testimony of contestant and witnesses, and in most cases the decision of the register and receiver. This series appears to include affidavits only for those cases in which the decision of the register and receiver was final. Affidavits for cases appealed to the commissioner of the General Land Office were apparently forwarded to the GLO.

Crookston Land District, 1886-1908. 4.5 c.f. (4 boxes and partial box)

Contest Affidavits

Affidavits filed by the Northern Pacific Railroad Company objecting to the allowance of preemption and homestead entries on certain land claimed by the railroad as part of its land grant.

The affidavits give the name of the entryman, legal description of the tract under dispute, date the land was selected by the Northern Pacific, and date the railroad filed objections to the entries made on the tract. Other documentation may include the application to enter land, homestead affidavit and receipts, and contest notices. Some affidavits are annotated to indicate the eventual disposition of the contest.

Duluth Land District, 1888-1889. 2 folders.

Contest Decisions

Copies of decisions rendered by the register and receiver on contested entries.

The register and receiver of the land office acted as arbiters in instances in which two or more individuals had filed claims to a parcel or in which an individual or the government challenged the validity of an entry. They took testimony from the contestants and witnesses and rendered their decision on the evidence presented. If the register and receiver differed in their verdict on a case, it was forwarded to the commissioner of the General Land Office for decision. Decisions of the register and receiver could also be appealed to the commissioner.

The contest decisions give the names of the contestant (plaintiff) and entryman (defendant); type and number of entry being contested; date the entry was made; grounds of the contest; a summary of the evidence presented including date of settlement, improvements made, and biographical information; and the decision of the register and receiver with supporting reasoning and citations.

Related Records: **Record of Letters Sent** (page 99); **Notices of Contest Decisions** (page 95).

Crookston Land District, 1899-1902. 0.5 c.f. (partial box)
Duluth Land District, 1904-1911. 0.5 c.f. (3 vols.)

Contest Docket

A summary record of official proceedings in contests brought against land entries in the various land districts.

The docket entry for each contest case includes the following information: names of plaintiff (contestant) and defendant (entryman), number of entry contested, legal description of the parcel covered by the contested entry, summary of actions taken on the case, and citations to decisions of the register and receiver or the commissioner of the General Land Office.

Arrangement: Chronological by date contest filed.
Finding Aids: Indexes in each volume.

Alexandria Land District, 1879-1883. 1 vol.
Cass Lake Land District, 1903-1908. 1.75 c.f. (5 vols.)
Crookston Land District, 1880-1913. 5.2 c.f. (15 vols.)
Duluth Land District, 1887-1888. 1 vol.
Minneapolis Land District, 1858-1867. Partial vol.
Red Wing Land District, 1872-1880. 1 vol.
Root River Land District, 1875-1879. 2 vols.
St. Cloud Land District, 1880-1888. 1 vol.
Stillwater Land District, 1883-1893. 1 vol.
Winona Land District, 1889-1898. 1 vol.

Contest Notices

Copies of letters sent to entrymen notifying them that a contest had been filed against their entries.

The contest notices include the following information: docket number, date a notice of contest was issued, name of person bringing the contest, entry number and date of entry of the contested claim, name of the entryman or defendant in the contest, grounds of the contest, and date set for a hearing before the register and receiver.

Related Records: **Record of Letters Sent** (page 99).

Crookston Land District, 1899-1906. 4 folders.

Correspondence, Miscellaneous

Miscellaneous letters received from the public and replies sent by the register and receiver. The letters received are mainly inquiries about the availability of land, procedures for entering land, the survey and entry of islands, and the status of entries.

Duluth Land District, 1920-1924. 4 folders.

Correspondence: Letters Received from GLO

Letters received by the register and receiver of each land district from the commissioner of the General Land Office. They include letters of transmission and acknowledgment, instructions to the register and receiver, decisions of the land commissioner and secretary of the interior in contested cases, and notices of approval or rejection of land entries.

The letters forwarding decisions of the commissioner and the secretary of the interior contain the most significant information. They generally include a summary of the facts in the case, giving information on the date of settlement and entry, improvements made on the claim, and biographical information on the contestants and witnesses. Some of these letters include transcripts of testimony and affidavits relating to the case.

Other letters focus on preemption, homestead, timber culture, Sioux and Chippewa half-breed scrip, military bounty land warrant, and cash entries for lands; railroad land grants; public land sales; timber trespass and fraudulent timber entries; and the general operation of the land offices. Topics discussed less frequently include other types of land entries; state swamp land and other grants; the grasshopper plagues of the 1870s; the survey and settlement of Indian land; Indian allotments and reservations; and colonization projects of Archbishop John Ireland.

Arrangement: Chronological.

Related Records: The **Original Entry Tract Books** (page 65) include citations, by date sent, to letters received from the commissioner of the GLO regarding specific parcels of land. See also **Record of Letters Received** (page 99).

Alexandria Land District, 1868-1889. 4.0 c.f. (4 boxes)
Crookston Land District, 1872-1908. 24.0 c.f. (24 boxes)
Duluth Land District, 1858-1908. 37.8 c.f. (38 boxes)
Minneapolis Land District, 1854-1889. 8.0 c.f. (8 boxes)
Red Wing Land District, 1855-1863, 1872-1889. 3.25 c.f. (3 boxes and partial box)
Root River Land District, 1854-1889. 9.0 c.f. (9 boxes)
St. Cloud Land District, 1853-1906. 25.0 c.f. (25 boxes)
Stillwater Land District, 1848-1893. 4.0 c.f. (4 boxes)
Winona Land District, 1854-1904. 19.0 c.f. (19 boxes)

Correspondence: Miscellaneous Letters Received

Letters received from private individuals, attorneys, land agents, and others. Most are requests for information on the availability of land for homesteading, on the status of entries or contested cases, or on regulations and procedures for perfecting homestead entries. Some letters give information on the dates homesteads were established and the improvements made, living conditions of homesteaders, and a variety of biographical data.

Crookston Land District, 1908-1912. 1.0 c.f. (1 box)

Correspondence: Receiver's Letters Sent

Copies of letters sent by the receivers of the various land districts in their capacities as receivers of public money and government disbursing agents.

Principal correspondents are the commissioner of the General Land Office, secretary of the treasury, and comptroller of the Treasury Department. The letters include transmittals of monthly and quarterly reports of accounts current and estimated office expenditures; inventories of office supplies and records; requests for information in procedural matters; responses to inquiries from the General Land Office or the Treasury Department about office receipts and expenditures; and reports on public auctions and the general operation of the land office. Occasional letters relate to contested entries.

Arrangement: Chronological.

Alexandria Land District, 1869-1880. 2 vols.
Crookston Land District, 1876-1908. 1.3 c.f. (11 vols.)
Duluth Land District, 1857-1911. 2.2 c.f. (17 vols.)
Minneapolis Land District, 1854-1883. 3 vols.
Red Wing Land District, 1854-1863, 1872-1889. 1 vol.
Root River Land District, 1854-1889. 1.2 c.f. (3 vols.)
St. Cloud Land District, 1853-1879. 2 vols.
Stillwater Land District, 1848-1893. 2 vols.
Winona Land District, 1854-1878. 2 vols.

Correspondence: Receiver's Miscellaneous Letters Sent

Letterpress copies of miscellaneous letters sent, largely to members of the public.

Many of the letters are answers to inquiries about the availability of land and procedures for entering land or to requests for plat maps and field notes. Others are responses to inquiries from special agents of the GLO investigating entries, letters to banks relating to deposits of land office money, and instructions to entrymen on correcting errors in their entries.

Duluth Land District, 1890-1907. 0.75 c.f. (6 vols.)

Correspondence: Register's Letters Sent

Handwritten and letterpress copies of outgoing letters of the registers of the various land districts. They are written primarily to the commissioner of the General Land Office, with some additional letters to federal and state officials and private citizens. Some letters of the receivers are included.

Letters to the GLO fall into two broad categories: routine interoffice communications and letters relating to imperfect or contested entries. The routine administrative correspondence includes letters of transmittal and acknowledgment, monthly and quarterly reports of entries made, record of patents delivered, requests for record books and forms, inquiries on procedural matters, and general commentary on the operation of the land office. The letters relating to contested entries include reports of the decisions of the register and receiver, accompanied by summaries of the facts and witnesses' testimony for those cases that were appealed to the commissioner of the GLO. In addition to naming the rival claimants and giving the legal description of the contested parcel, these letters often cite the date of settlement and entry, describe the improvements made--sometimes in great detail—and give biographical information on the contestants and witnesses in the case. The letters concerning imperfect entries are usually responses to requests from the commissioner for additional information needed to approve an entry. This most often relates to the entryman's naturalization, change in name, witnesses' testimony, or procedural matters.

The series includes occasional letters to registers of other land offices and to the U.S. Surveyor General, and a few letters to the governor or state land commissioner relating to state land grants.

Letters to private individuals consist primarily of notices of hearings set, appeals forwarded, or decisions rendered in contested cases; requests for additional information or testimony; and procedural instructions necessary to perfect an entry.

Among the topics covered in the letters sent are: homestead and preemption claims, military bounty land warrant entries, railroad land grants, Sioux half-breed scrip entries, townsite locations, public land sales, and state land grants.

Arrangement: Chronological.

Alexandria Land District, 1869-1881. 3 vols.
Crookston Land District, 1872-1913. 6.0 c.f. (54 vols.)
Duluth Land District, 1857-1873. 1 vol.
Housed in Northeast Minnesota Historical Center, Duluth.
Duluth Land District, 1873-1911. 13.0 c.f. (89 vols.)
Minneapolis Land District, 1854-1878. 1.5 c.f. (6 vols.)
Red Wing Land District, 1855-1889. 1.5 c.f. (4 vols.)
Root River Land District, 1854-1886. 2.0 c.f. (6 vols.)
St. Cloud Land District, 1860-1879. 1.3 c.f. (4 vols.)
Stillwater Land District, 1848-1893. 1.7 c.f. (5 vols.)
Winona Land District, 1857-1869. 1 vol. and partial vol.

Correspondence: Register's Miscellaneous Letters Sent

Letterpress copies of letters sent to private individuals, attorneys, land agents, and special investigating agents of the General Land Office. Some receiver's letters are included also.

Letters to private individuals include replies to requests for information on the availability of land, the status of entries and contest cases, and procedures for making various types of land entries; instructions to entrymen on perfecting erroneous applications to enter land; and discussions of alleged illegal cutting of timber on public land. Letters to special agents of the GLO explain cases in which the register was asking the special agent to investigate "suspicious proofs" made by entrymen, giving details of the entry and the reasons for questioning the proof.

Arrangement: Chronological.

Crookston Land District, 1897-1908. 9.0 c.f. (69 vols. and 1 folder)
Duluth Land District, 1900-1911. 3.0 c.f. (19 vols.)

Homestead Final Proofs

A fragmentary series of final proofs made on homestead entries in the Winona land district.

Homesteaders were required to submit a "final proof" to the local land office demonstrating that they had complied with the requirements of the Homestead Act and were entitled to receive a final certificate on their claim. The homestead final proofs include the following information: final certificate number; homestead entry number; name of homesteader; legal description of the tract covered by the entry; date residence on the homestead began; description of the improvements made on the claim including the house, outbuildings, fences, and crops and trees planted; and date proof was made. The proof may also include a variety of biographical information.

Winona Land District, 1870, 1879. 2 folders.

Indian Traders' Applications to Enter Land

Applications of licensed Indian traders to enter land in the Duluth land district under provisions of the Chippewa Treaty of La Pointe of September 30, 1854.

The tenth article of the treaty allowed licensed traders and some craftsmen to enter the land on which they had established their posts or shops. The applications give the name of the trader making application, tract applied for, date of settlement on the tract, and date a license was issued.

Duluth Land District, 1857-1858. 1 folder.

List of Forfeited Homesteads

A list of homestead entries on which five-year and seven-year forfeiture notices were issued under terms of the General Land Office circular of December 20, 1873.

Homestead entrants could "prove up" their claim five years after the date of entry and were expected to make final proof within seven years. By the circular of December 20, 1873, the register was to notify the homesteader that his entry would be canceled unless proved up or otherwise perfected. The seven year notice gave the homesteader a final opportunity to make final proof or commute the homestead to a cash, scrip, or warrant entry.

The list includes the following information: date the notice was issued, date of entry, entry number, name of homesteader, legal description of the tract homesteaded, and acreage of the homestead. Most of the seven year notices include citations to commissioner's letters or various registers of entries.

Red Wing Land District, 1873-1877. Partial vol.

List of Land Offered for Sale

A list of land offered for sale at public auction at the Forest City land office of the Minneapolis land district on October 15, 1860.

The land was in townships 121-124, ranges 34-36. No bids were received. The register's letter sent of November 5, 1860, discusses the sale and allegations of conspiracies to withhold bids on the offered land.

Minneapolis Land District, 1860. 1 vol.

List of Land Sold: Chippewa Pine Land

A list of ceded Chippewa pine land offered for sale at public auction under provisions of acts of January 14, 1889, and February 26, 1896.

The list records land offered at auction on July 1, 1896, and August 2, 1898, and includes the following information for each parcel: legal description, appraised value, purchaser's name, entry number (recorded in **Register of Certificates to Purchasers: Chippewa Land** (described on page 102), and purchase price, or "no bid" if the parcel was not sold.

Duluth Land District, 1896-1898. 1 folder.

List of Patents for Winnebago Land

Lists of patents issued to purchasers of land in the former Winnebago Indian reservation on the Blue Earth River in Blue Earth and Waseca counties.

The Winnebago reservation--consisting of townships 106-107, ranges 24-27; sections 31-36 of township 108, ranges 24-27; and sections 6, 7, 18, 19, 30 and 31 of townships 106-107, range 23--was set aside for the Winnebago Indians by the treaty of February 27, 1855, in which the Winnebago ceded title to the Long Prairie Reservation in Todd County in exchange for the Blue Earth Reservation. The Blue Earth Reservation was opened for entry by an act of February 21, 1863, "for the removal of the Winnebago Indians and for the sale of their reservation."

The lists give the name of the person to whom each patent was issued, legal description of the tract patented, and date the patent was issued. Not all of the patents recorded in these lists are recorded in the GLO Tract Books.

Related Records: **Register of Certificates to Purchasers: Winnebago Land** (pages 103-104).

Winona Land District, 1865-1878. 1 folder.

List of Suspended Homestead Entries

A list of homestead entries that were suspended or rejected for failure of the entryman to fulfill the conditions of the Homestead Act.

The list includes the following information for each suspended entry: homestead entry number, name of the entryman, legal description of the tract covered, and occasional notes on the re-entry of the parcel citing the name and residence of the person making re-entry.

The list of suspended homestead entries is recorded on forms for military bounty land warrant entries.

Root River Land District, 1864-1869. 1 folder.

List of Suspended Preemption Entries

A list of preemption entries suspended by the commissioner of the General Land Office pending presentation of additional proofs and explanations.

The list includes the following information: citation to commissioner's letter suspending the preemption entry, name of individual whose entry was suspended, number of the preemption declaratory statement and/or number of the certificate to purchaser, and citation to the register's letter in which the additional proof was forwarded to the GLO.

Winona Land District, 1855-1861. 1 vol.

Lists of Land Offered for Sale

An incomplete series of lists of land offered for sale at public auction. Public auctions were held in October and November, 1860; August 15, 1864; December 16, 1872; January 13, 1873; January 15, 1883; and August 20, 1883.

The records list each parcel offered at auction by range, township, section, and fractional section. Very few of the parcels offered were sold at auction; most are annotated "no bid." Parcels that were sold at auction are recorded in the **Register of Certificates to Purchasers** (pages 101-102) under the date of the sale and are marked as "public sale" entries.

St. Cloud Land District, 1860-1883. 0.75 c.f. (11 vols.)

Miscellaneous Records

Miscellaneous documents filed in support of land entries. They include several copies of naturalization records, proofs of military service, and a proof of right to preempt land.

Alexandria Land District, 1878-1885. 1 folder.

Miscellaneous Records

Inventories of office records and furnishings (1885-1906), list of attorneys admitted to practice before the land office, applications for leave of absence (1896-1902), and relinquishments of preference rights (1908-1920).

Crookston Land District, 1885-1920. 5 folders.

Notices of Contest Decisions

Letterpress copies of notices sent to parties in contested entry cases informing them about the status of their claims. Some merely state that the commissioner's decision had been received at the land office and that the entryman had a specified amount of time in which to file an appeal. Others give a summary of the facts in the case, particularly in cases involving soldiers' additional homestead rights.

Duluth Land District, 1904-1911. 3.0 c.f. (18 vols.)

Proof Right to Preemption

Proofs of right to make preemption entries filed on land in the Mille Lacs Indian reservation. These proofs were rejected and the entries canceled by the commissioner's letter of January 24, 1872.

The preemption proofs give the name of the preempting settler, description of the tract settled, and date settled. The statements of two witnesses testify to the preemptor's residence on the tract and the extent of the improvements made on the claim.

Stillwater Land District, 1871. 1 folder.

Receiver's Abstracts of Collections

A record of money collected by the receiver as the purchase price and/or fees for various types of land entries.

The abstracts for each type of entry were recorded separately and include: homestead entries, final homestead certificates, railroad selections, Valentine scrip entries, soldier's homestead declaratory statements, homestead entries for Chippewa land, public sales entries, timber and stone entries, private cash entries, installment payments on homestead entries on ceded Chippewa land, and cash purchases of excesses on warrant and scrip entries.

The abstract for each payment received includes the following information: date received, serial register number, receipt number, name of person making payment, rate per acre, and fees and commissions paid.

Duluth Land District, 1908-1913. 1 vol.

Receiver's Accounts as Disbursing Agent

Quarterly accounts of the receiver acting in his capacity as disbursing agent for federal funds.

The accounts itemize expenditures for salaries, office supplies and furniture, commissions and fees paid to the register and receiver, and incidental expenses incurred in the operation of the land office.

Cass Lake Land District, June 1903-April 1909. 1 vol.
Crookston Land District, 1872-1908. 3 vols.

Receiver's Accounts of Transcribing Fees

Detailed monthly accounts of fees received for reducing testimony to writing in contest cases or for testimony accompanying entries made under the Desert Land Act, Timber Culture Act, or other specified acts, and for making copies of plats.

The accounts give the date payment was received, name of the person making payment, law under which the entry was made, entry number, and amount received.

Cass Lake Land District, July 1903-June 1908. 1 vol.
Crookston Land District, 1892-1907. 2 vols.

Receiver's Accounts of Unearned Fees

Detailed monthly records and quarterly accounts of "unearned fees and unofficial monies" received for applications which had been disallowed, deposited as fees for notices in contest cases, or received as security deposits for transcribing testimony in contest cases.

A General Land Office circular in volume 1 for each district explains the procedures the receiver was to follow in accounting for unearned fees.

Cass Lake Land District, 1903-1908. 2 vols.
Crookston Land District, 1895-1908. 0.6 c.f. (5 vols.)

Receiver's Estimates of Office Expenditures

An incomplete series of the receiver's yearly estimates of the expenses to be incurred in operating the land office during the following fiscal year. The estimates include salary of register and receiver, cost of hiring clerks and other office staff, expenses for conducting public auctions of land, binding volumes of records, and printing various notices in newspapers, and other miscellaneous expenses.

Winona Land District, 1854-1864. 1 folder.

Receiver's Miscellaneous Accounts

Various accounts and records of monies received, consisting of abstracts of receipts (July 1912-June 1919), abstracts of collections and expenditures in contested cases (1908-1913), abstracts of monies returned or applied (July 1912-Dec. 1913), abstracts of unearned fees received (April 1909-June 1912), abstracts of unearned fees returned (July 1908-June 1912), abstract of treasury deposits (July 1908-July 1912), recapitulation of abstracts of collections (1908-1912), and receiver's accounts current (1908-1916).

Duluth Land District, 1908-1916. 0.4 c.f. (8 folders)

Receiver's Monthly Accounts Current

Summary monthly accounts of money received from the sale of public land and from fees and commissions received for homestead, warrant, and scrip entries. The monthly accounts record the totals of cash received from various sources by the receiver and the amounts deposited in banks in account with the United States.

Cass Lake Land District, July 1903-June 1908. 1 vol.
Crookston Land District, 1885-1908. 3 vols.

Receiver's Monthly Statement of Earned Fees

Monthly summary record of fees and commissions received for homestead, timber culture, warrant, and scrip entries; preemption declaratory statements filed; railroad selection lists filed; and other services performed by the register and receiver.

Records for each month give the number of entries in each category, inclusive entry numbers, total acreage embraced in the entries for each category, and total fees paid on each type of entry, statement, and selection list.

Cass Lake Land District, July 1903-June 1908. 1 vol.
Crookston Land District, 1885-June 1908. 1 vol.

Receiver's Quarterly Accounts Current

Receiver's quarterly detailed and summary accounts of money received from the sale of public land and for fees and commissions received for various types of land entries.

The detailed accounts record all money received for land sold, giving date of sale, receipt number, purchaser's name, description of the tract sold, price per acre, and notes on the type of entry (e.g., public or private sale, excess on warrant or scrip entries, or commuted homestead entry). Totals for fees and commissions received are recorded, as are all deposits made in account with the United States.

The summary accounts provide totals for each quarter's receipts and balances.

Cass Lake Land District, 1903-1907. 2 vols.
Crookston Land District, 1872-1908. 1.5 c.f. (5 vols.)
Red Wing Land District, Nov. 1855-Feb. 1856. 1 folder.

Record of Application to Make Final Proof

A record of applications to make final proof on homestead and Timber and Stone Act entries.

The record of each application includes the following information: type of entry, entry number, date of entry, name and residence of entryman, legal description of the tract to be "proved up," date of application to make proof, person before whom proof is to be made, where proof is to be made, date set for proof, newspaper in which proof is to be announced, date proof was actually made, and action taken by the register and receiver (proof accepted or rejected).

Arrangement: Chronological by date application filed.

Cass Lake Land District, Dec. 1914-July 1926. 1 vol.
Crookston Land District, 1905-June 1908. 1 vol.

Record of Applications for Refunds

A record of applications from entrymen for repayment of monies paid to or deposited with the receiver for land entries that were later rejected or withdrawn.

The record of applications gives the type and number of the entry in question, name of the entryman, tract covered by the entry, date the application was filed with the land office, date the request was transmitted to the commissioner of the General Land Office, and citations to the commissioner's letter ruling on the application.

Crookston Land District, 1887-1910. 1 vol.

Record of Canceled Homestead Entries

A record of homestead entries that were canceled by the commissioner of the General Land Office or relinquished by the entryman.

The record includes the following information for each canceled homestead entry: entry number and series, date the entry was filed, name of entryman, tract covered by the canceled entry, and date the entry was canceled by commissioner's letter or relinquishment.

Arrangement: Chronological by date of cancelation.

Cass Lake Land District, 1906-1908. 1 vol.
Crookston Land District, 1905-1908. 1 vol.

Record of Daily Cash Receipts and Balances

Daily record of money received for cash entries, and for fees and commissions received for declaratory statements and homestead, timber culture, warrant, and scrip entries. It lists the entry number and type and the amount of money received for each transaction, with daily balances.

A General Land Office circular, located at the beginning of volume 2 of the Crookston daily record, explains the procedure receivers were to follow in recording the daily cash receipts.

Cass Lake Land District, 1903-1908. 2 vols.
Crookston Land District, 1885-1908. 2.7 c.f. (11 vols.)

Record of Letters Received

An abstract of letters received from the commissioner of the General Land Office.

The abstract of each letter received includes the following information: letter number (assigned chronologically by the receiving land office), GLO identification initial, date of letter, name of person/case discussed in the letter, a brief of the subject of the letter, date the letter was received, date the letter was answered and/or a notice was sent to the entryman, and a summary of the actions taken in response to the commissioner's letter.

Arrangement: Chronological by date letter received.

Related Records: **Correspondence: Letters Received from GLO** (page 89).

Cass Lake Land District, 1903-1909. 3 vols.
Crookston Land District, 1896-1910. 1.75 c.f. (6 vols.)
St. Cloud Land District, 1901-1904. 1 vol.

Record of Letters Sent

An abstract of letters sent to parties involved in contested cases announcing the decision of the local land officers or the commissioner of the General Land Office.

The record includes the following information: date the letter was sent, person to whom sent, subject of the letter, "limit" or date before which a response must be filed, and citations to letters from the commissioner of the General Land Office relating to the subject.

Related Records: **Correspondence: Letters Received from GLO** (page 89); **Correspondence: Register's Letters Sent** (page 91); **Contest Notices** (page 88).

Crookston Land District, 1886-1917. 3 vols.

Record of Miscellaneous Applications

A record of applications filed to amend a homestead entry, make a second homestead entry, take leave of absence from a homestead, purchase an isolated tract, or file a protest against a homestead entry.

The record for each application lists the application number, type of application, tract involved in the application, name of the applicant, date of application, and remarks on the granting or rejection of the application with occasional citations to letters from the commissioner of the General Land Office or to the **Contest Docket** (page 88). The applications for leave of absence from a homestead were recorded separately in volume 1 of the series **Record of Rejected and Suspended Applications and Proofs** (below) between January, 1897, and June, 1902, but then were recorded consecutively with the other miscellaneous applications.

Crookston Land District, 1896-1909. 1.0 c.f. (2 vols. and partial vol.)

Record of Patents Delivered

Record of patents delivered to patentees or their agents for land entered in the various land districts.

The record gives the type and number of entry, person to whom the patent was issued, date the patent was issued, volume and page where the patent is recorded in GLO records, and name and address of the person to whom the patent was delivered.

Arrangement: Roughly chronological by date delivered.
Finding Aids: Indexed by name of patentee.

Alexandria Land District, 1884-1889. 1 vol.
Cass Lake Land District, 1903-1914 (bulk 1904-1908). 2 vols.
Crookston Land District, 1878-1911. 2 vols.
Duluth Land District, 1861-1908. 1.3 c.f. (4 vols.)
Minneapolis Land District, July 1884-Feb. 1889. 1 vol.
Red Wing Land District, Aug. 1884-Feb. 1889. 1 vol.
Root River Land District, 1884-1889. 1 vol.
St. Cloud Land District, 1884-1907. 1 vol.
Stillwater Land District, Aug. 1884-Dec. 1893. 1 vol.
Winona Land District, 1884-1903. 1 vol.

Record of Rejected and Suspended Applications and Proofs

A record of applications to enter land and of final homestead proofs that were rejected or suspended by the register and receiver or the commissioner of the General Land Office.

The record for each rejected/suspended entry or proof includes the following information; rejection/suspension number, description of the tract covered by the application or proof, name of the person applying to enter land or make final proof, date of suspension/rejection, and remarks on the grounds for suspension/rejection. Some include citations to letters from the commissioner of the General Land Office and notes on the eventual disposition of the entry. Applications to enter land and final proofs that were suspended by the register and receiver were usually forwarded to the commissioner of the General Land Office for final decision.

Arrangement: Chronological.
Finding Aids: Volumes indexed by name of applicant/entryman.
Related Records: **Rejected Applications to Enter Land** (page 112); **Rejected Homestead Proofs** (page 112).

Cass Lake Land District, 1902-1908. 1 vol.
Crookston Land District, 1896-1908. 1.7 c.f. (4 vols. and partial vol.)

Register of Agricultural College Scrip Entries

An abstract of land entries made with agricultural college scrip under provisions of the Agricultural College Act of 1862.

The Agricultural College Act, commonly referred to as the Morrill Act, granted each state 30,000 acres of land for each of its United States senators and representatives. The proceeds from the sale of this land were to be used for the benefit of colleges of agricultural and mechanical arts. Those states in which public land was still available for private entry selected their grants from the public land within their boundaries. Those states without sufficient public land received scrip of equal value which could be redeemed for public land in the western states. The states receiving scrip could not enter the land directly but were required to sell the scrip to second parties who then used it to locate land or resold it.

The abstract for each scrip entry includes the following information: land office entry number, scrip number, date a scrip certificate was issued, to what state the scrip was issued, acre value of the scrip, legal description of the tract located with the scrip, date located, and by whom located, with occasional added remarks.

Arrangement: Chronological by date scrip located (certificate issued).

Crookston Land District, June 1872-April 1897. 1 vol.
Minneapolis Land District, 1863-1873. 1 vol.
Red Wing Land District, 1864-1872. 1 folder
Root River Land District, 1863-1875. 1 vol.
St. Cloud Land District, April 1864-Nov. 1887. Partial vol.
Stillwater Land District, 1864-1872. 1 vol.
Winona Land District, June 1864-May 1892. 2 vols.

Register of Certificates to Purchasers

An abstract of certificates issued by the register of the land office for land entries made by cash purchase. The certificate established the buyer's legal claim to a parcel of land pending issuance by the GLO of a patent that formally transferred title.

The abstract for each certificate includes the following information: certificate number, date issued, name of purchaser and county of residence, legal description of the parcel purchased, total acreage of the parcel, price per acre, and total purchase price. Most abstracts are annotated with the date the patent was issued and the volume and page in which it is recorded in GLO patent records. A few include citations to letters from the commissioner of the General Land Office.

Included in this series is the receiver's register of receipts for cash entries, which essentially duplicates information in the register of certificates except for occasional differences in the annotations.

Arrangement: By chronologically assigned certificate number.
Related Records: **Register of Final Homestead Certificates** (page 104); **Register of Homestead Entries** (pages 106-107); **Register of Certificates to Purchasers: Winnebago Land** (pages 103-104).

Alexandria Land District, 1869-1889. 1 vol.
Cass Lake Land District, 1903-1908. 2 vols.
Crookston Land District, 1872-1908. 1.9 c.f. (6 vols.)
Duluth Land District, 1857-1908. 2.5 c.f. (6 vols.)
Minneapolis Land District, 1866-1879. 2 vols.
Red Wing Land District, 1855-1863, 1872-1889. 0.7 c.f. (5 vols. and 1 folder)
Root River Land District, 1854-1886. 1.2 c.f. (4 vols.)
St. Cloud Land District, 1853-1906. 1.5 c.f. (4 vols.)
Stillwater Land District, 1875-1893. 1 vol.
Winona Land District, 1855-1903. 1.0 c.f. (5 vols.)

Register of Certificates to Purchasers: Chippewa Land

An abstract of certificates issued for land entries made by cash purchase for ceded Chippewa reservation land, under provisions of the Nelson Act of January 14, 1889.

This act, named for Minnesota congressman Knute Nelson, called for the Chippewa to cede all their reservation land in Minnesota except the Red Lake and White Earth reservations. All Chippewa except the Red Lake Band were then to be concentrated on the White Earth Reservation and given allotments in severalty. The Red Lake Indians were to receive their allotments on the Red Lake Reservation. Land in excess of that needed to provide allotments for the enrolled tribal members was to be ceded to the government, surveyed, and appraised as agricultural or timber land. The agricultural land was to be opened for entry by "purchased homestead" and the timber land was to be sold at public auction with all proceeds placed in trust for the Chippewa.

Under the Nelson Act, homesteads on ceded Chippewa land had to be purchased at the rate of $1.25 per acre with payments due in five equal installments. Residence requirements and "proving up" procedures were the same as for regular homesteads. Originally the homesteads on Chippewa land could not be commuted but a later amendment allowed them to be commuted to cash entries. The procedure for making cash entries on the ceded Chippewa land was the same as for cash entries on public land except that the minimum price was based on the appraised value of the timber on the land.

The abstract for each certificate includes the following information: certificate number, date issued, legal description of the parcel purchased, name of purchaser, total acreage of the parcel, appraised value, price per acre, and total purchase price. Most abstracts are annotated with the date the patent was issued and the volume and page in which it is recorded in GLO patent records. Some include citations to letters from the commissioner of the General Land Office. The series also records installment and commutation payments for homestead entries on ceded Chippewa land.

Included in this series is the receiver's register of receipts for cash entries, which essentially duplicates information in the register of certificates except for occasional differences in the annotations.

Arrangement: By chronologically assigned certificate number.

Related Records: **Register of Final Homestead Certificates: Chippewa Land** (page 105); **Register of Homestead Entries: Chippewa Land** (page 107); **List of Land Sold: Chippewa Pine Land** (page 93).

Cass Lake Land District, 1903-1908. 2 vols.
Crookston Land District, 1896-1908. 1.25 c.f. (4 vols.)
Duluth Land District, 1896-1908. 1 vol.

Register of Certificates to Purchasers: Sioux Land

Abstracts of cash entries made for land in the former Sioux Indian reservation.

A reservation for the Sioux Indians had been established along the Minnesota River by the Treaty of 1851. In the aftermath of the Dakota War of 1862 the Indians were removed and the land was opened for purchase.

The register records the following information for each entry: legal description of the tract purchased, acreage of the tract, price per acre, total purchase price, name of purchaser, date of purchase, certificate number, person to whom patented, date the patent was issued, and volume and page where the patent is recorded in GLO records.

Included in this series is the receiver's register of receipts for cash entries, which essentially duplicates information in the register of certificates, except for occasional differences in the annotations.

Arrangement: Chronological by date of purchase.

Minneapolis Land District, 1869-1902. 0.9 c.f. (5 vols.)
Red Wing Land District, 1872-1889. 1 vol.
Winona Land District, 1865-1869. 3 vols.

Register of Certificates to Purchasers: Winnebago Land

An abstract of cash entries made in the Winona land district for land in the former Winnebago Indian reservation on the Blue Earth River.

The register includes the following information for each entry: certificate number; date the land was sold; name and residence of purchaser; legal description of the parcel purchased; acreage of the parcel; price per acre, total price, and annotations giving the date a patent was issued; volume and page in GLO records where it is recorded; and citations to letters from the commissioner of the General Land Office.

This register is included in volume 2 of the Winona district's **Register of Certificates to Purchasers** (page 101). Entry nos. 165-448 (May 1, 1865-Nov. 20, 1878) were recorded separately from the sale of public land and are found at the end of the volume. Prior to that time (Oct. 3, 1864-April 27, 1865), entries for Winnebago land were recorded and numbered consecutively with other cash entries and denoted by the annotation "Win Res" and an additional entry number (1-164); they are found between Register of Certificates entry nos. 5783 and 6025.

Related Records: **List of Patents for Winnebago Land** (page 93).

Winona Land District, 1864-1878. Partial vol.

Register of Chippewa Half-Breed Scrip Entries

Abstracts of land entries made with Chippewa half-breed scrip.

The treaty of September 20, 1854, between the Lake Superior Chippewa and the United States and the treaty of April 7, 1866, between the Bois Fort Chippewa and the United States reserved tracts of land for Chippewa half-breeds. The half-breeds did not take up this land and eventually it was opened for entry. Half-breed title to the tract was extinguished by dividing the reserves among the enrolled half-breeds and issuing scrip to each individual in proportion to his or her share of the reserve. By law the scrip could not be alienated, but this restriction was often evaded and much of the scrip was entered by someone other than the person to whom it was issued.

The abstract for each scrip entry includes the following information: entry number, scrip number, date the scrip was issued, person to whom issued, person by whom the scrip was located, date located, legal description of the tract located, and occasional remarks with citations to letters from the commissioner of the General Land Office.

Arrangement: Chronological by date the scrip was located.

Duluth Land District, 1858-1880. 1 folder
Winona Land District, 1864. 1 vol.

Register of Final Homestead Certificates

An abstract of all final certificates issued for homesteaded land in each land district.

The abstract for each final certificate includes the following information: final certificate number; date the certificate was filed; legal description of the tract homesteaded; name of the applicant and county of residence; number of the original homestead application (recorded in **Register of Homestead Entries**, pages 106-107); commissions and fees paid; price per acre (commissions were based on the appraised price per acre); and various remarks relative to delivery of patents, citations to letters from the commissioner of the General Land Office, and citations to the **Register of Certificates to Purchasers** (pages 101-102) if the acreage of the parcel originally entered was in excess of the applicant's homestead eligibility.

Some land districts maintained separate registers of receipts for the commissions and fees paid by the receiver in conjunction with the issuance of final homestead certificates. Except for occasional differences in the annotations, they essentially duplicate information in the Register of Final Homestead Certificates, and are treated as a subset of this series.

Arrangement: Chronological by date the final certificate was issued.

Alexandria Land District, 1869-1889. 1 vol.
Cass Lake Land District, 1903-1908. 2 vols.
Crookston Land District, 1873-1908. 2.4 c.f. (6 vols.)
Duluth Land District, 1868-1908. 1.5 c.f. (4 vols.)
Minneapolis Land District, 1868-1889. 2 vols.
Red Wing Land District, 1868-1889. 0.75 c.f. (3 vols.)
Root River Land District, 1868-1889. 2 vols.
St. Cloud Land District, 1868-1906. 1.2 c.f. (3 vols.)
Stillwater Land District, 1868-1893. 2 vols.
Winona Land District, 1868-1903. 3 vols.

Register of Final Homestead Certificates: Chippewa Land

An abstract of final homestead certificates for entries made on ceded Chippewa reservation land under provisions of the Homestead Act of 1862 and the Nelson Act of January 14, 1889.

Final certificates for homesteads on ceded Chippewa land were issued after the entryman had proved up his claim, demonstrating compliance with the residency requirements as in regular homestead entries, and had paid for his homestead as provided for by the Nelson Act.

The abstract for each final certificate includes the following information: final certificate number, date the certificate was issued, legal description of the tract homesteaded, name of the entryman, number of the original homestead entry (recorded in the **Register of Homestead Entries: Chippewa Land**) and occasional remarks with citations to letters received from the commissioner of the General Land Office.

Included in this series is the receiver's register of final homestead receipts for Chippewa land, which essentially duplicates information in the register of final certificates except for occasional differences in the annotations.

Arrangement: Chronological.

Related Records: **Register of Homestead Entries: Chippewa Land** (page 107); **Register of Certificates to Purchasers: Chippewa Land** (pages 102-103).

Cass Lake Land District, 1903-1908. 2 vols.
Crookston Land District, 1899-1908. 2 vols.
Duluth Land District, 1903-1904. 1 folder.

Register of Final Timber Culture Certificates

An abstract of final certificates for land entered under provisions the Timber Culture Act of 1873.

The intent of the Timber Culture Act was to encourage the planting of trees on the western prairies. The law enabled qualified individuals to acquire title to 160 acres of land on the condition that forty acres be planted to trees. Residence on the tract was not required. In the original act the entryman was required to plant the entire 40 acres to trees in the first year after making entry. The time period was later extended to four years, and in 1878 the acreage was reduced to ten acres with a minimum of 2700 trees per acre at the time of planting and "675 living, thrifty trees" at the time of patenting. Timber culture entries could be "proved up" and patented after eight years. They could be made in addition to homestead or preemption entries. The Timber Culture Act was repealed in 1891.

The abstract for each final certificate includes the following information: final certificate number, date the certificate was issued, legal description of the tract on which the certificate was issued, name and residence of the entryman, number of the original timber culture entry, fees paid, and occasional remarks with citations to letters received from the commissioner of the General Land Office.

Included in this series is the register of final timber culture receipts. The final receipt was issued by the receiver of the land office to the entryman for money received in payment of fees and commissions. The register of final receipts contains the same information as the register of final certificates, except that there may be occasional differences in the annotations.

Related Records: **Register of Timber Culture Entries** (page 111).

Crookston Land District, 1884-1903. 0.7 c.f. (4 vols.)

Register of Forest Reserve Lieu Entries

An abstract of entries (nos. 1-839) made with forest reserve lieu scrip.

The Forest Reserve Lieu Act of June 4, 1897, allowed settlers or owners of unperfected or patented claims in established forest reserves to relinquish such claims and select, in lieu, vacant land open for settlement in an amount equal to that relinquished.

The abstract for each lieu entry includes the following information: entry number, date entered, name of entryman, legal description of the tract entered, selection number, forest reserve tract relinquished and in lieu of which the entry was made, and occasional annotations with citations to letters received from the commissioner of the General Land Office.

Duluth Land District, Sept. 1900-Jan. 1905. 1 vol.

Register of Homestead Entries

An abstract of all applications to acquire land under the provisions of the Homestead Act of 1862 that were filed in the various land districts.

The abstract for each homestead entry includes the following information: number of the application or declaratory statement; date of application; name of the applicant; legal description of the parcel entered; and remarks on the issuance of a patent, cancelation, or other disposition of the entry, with citations to relevant letters from the commissioner of the General Land Office.

Included in this series is the receiver's register of homestead entry receipts, for fees and commissions paid by the homesteader at the time of entry. It essentially duplicates the information in the Register of Homestead Entries, except for occasional differences in the annotations.

Arrangement: By chronologically assigned application (entry) number.

Alexandria Land District, 1863-1889. 2 vols.
Cass Lake Land District, 1903-1908. 2 vols.
Crookston Land District, 1872-1908. 3.0 c.f. (8 vols.)
Duluth Land District, 1863-1908. 3.0 c.f. (8 vols.)
Minneapolis Land District, 1863-1889. 1.5 c.f. (6 vols.)
Red Wing Land District, 1862-1889. 1.0 c.f. (3 vols.)
Root River Land District, 1863-1889. 1.8 c.f. (5 vols.)
St. Cloud Land District, 1863-1906. 1.75 c.f. (5 vols.)
Stillwater Land District, 1863-1893. 1.25 c.f. (3 vols.)
Winona Land District, 1863-1903. 1.5 c.f. (11 vols.)

Register of Homestead Entries: Chippewa Land

An abstract of homestead entries on ceded Chippewa reservation land made under provisions of the Homestead Act of 1862 and the Nelson Act of January 14, 1889 (see page 102).

The abstract for each homestead entry includes the following information: entry number, date of entry, legal description of the tract entered, name and residence of the entryman, fees and commissions paid, and occasional notes on the eventual disposition of the entry with citations to letters received from the commissioner of the General Land Office.

Included in this series is the receiver's register of homestead entry receipts, for fees and commission's paid by the homesteader at the time of entry. It essentially duplicates the information in the Register of Homestead Entries, except for occasional differences in the annotations.

Arrangement: By chronologically assigned entry number.

Related Records: **Register of Certificates to Purchasers: Chippewa Land** (pages 102-103); **Register of Final Homestead Certificates: Chippewa Land** (page 105).

Cass Lake Land District, 1903-1908. 2 vols.
Crookston Land District, 1896-1908. 2.0 c.f. (6 vols.)
Duluth Land District, 1896-1908. 2 vols.

Register of Indian Allotment Entries: Dawes Act

Abstracts of land entries made under provisions of the Indian Allotment Act of February 8, 1887.

The Indian Allotment Act, often referred to as the Dawes Act, provided for the breaking up of Indian reservations by allotting land in severalty to individual Indians and opening the excess of reservation land to settlement. Land "suitable for agricultural and grazing purposes" was to be allotted in tracts of 160 acres to all heads of families, 80 acres to all single persons over 18 and orphan children under 18, and 40 acres to all other children. All land beyond that needed to provide allotments for the enrolled tribal members was to be opened for settlement.

The Register of Indian Allotment Entries records the applications of Indians to receive their allotted acreage as provided for in the Dawes Act. The abstract for each allotment entry includes the following information: application number, date of application, name and tribal affiliation of applicant and/or minor child, description of the tract applied for, and remarks on the disposition or cancellation of the entry with citations to letters from the commissioner of the General Land Office.

Arrangement: By chronologically assigned application number.

Crookston Land District, 1893-1897. 1 vol.
Duluth Land District, 1888-1908. 3 vols.
St. Cloud Land District, 1889-1902. 1 vol.

Register of Indian Allotment Entries: Nelson Act

Abstracts of land entries made on Indian allotments in Chippewa reservations under provisions of the Nelson Act of January 14, 1889 (see page 102).

The abstract for each allotment entry includes the following information: allotment number, Indian and/or English name of the allottee, tribal band of the allottee, legal description of the tract covered by the allotment, and other identifying information.

Crookston Land District, 1901. 1 vol.
Duluth Land District, 1896-1897. 2 folders.

Register of Military Bounty Land Warrant Entries

Registers or abstracts of public land entries made with military bounty land warrants.

Under acts of 1842, 1847, 1850, 1852, and 1855, Congress authorized the issuance of land warrants as a bounty for military service. The warrants entitled the holder to enter or "locate" a specified amount of public land. The warrants were transferable and most were entered by someone other than the person to whom they were originally issued.

The abstract for each warrant entry includes the land office entry number, warrant number, date the warrant was issued, person in whose favor the warrant was issued, legal description of the tract located with the warrant, date located, and by whom located. Some entries are annotated with citations to decisions of the commissioner of the General Land Office.

Arrangement: By warrant type, thereunder chronological by date of land office entry.

Alexandria Land District, 1869-1888. 3 vols.
Cass Lake Land District, 1904-1905. 1 folder.

Crookston Land District, 1873-1888. 1 vol.
Duluth Land District, 1857-1908. 2 vols. and 1 folder.
Minneapolis Land District, 1855-1880. 3 folders.
Red Wing Land District, 1855-1863. 2.0 c.f. (7 vols.)
Root River Land District, 1854-1880. 1.25 c.f. (5 vols.)
St. Cloud Land District, 1853-1906. 1 vol.
Winona Land District, 1855-1895. 0.9 c.f. (7 vols.)

Register of Red Lake and Pembina Scrip Entries

An abstract of land entries made with Red Lake and Pembina scrip. The authorization for this scrip is not specified on the abstract, but it probably pertains to cessions under treaties with the Red Lake and Pembina bands of Chippewa of 1863 and/or 1867.

The abstract for each scrip entry includes the following information: entry number, scrip number, person to whom the scrip was issued, legal description of the tract entered with the scrip, date the tract was entered, person who located the scrip, and occasional remarks with citations to letters from the commissioner of the General Land Office.

The records are photostatic copies of originals that were sent to the General Land Office.

Crookston Land District, 1873-1906. 1 folder.

Register of Sioux Half-Breed Scrip Entries

Abstracts of land entries made with Sioux half-breed scrip.

The Treaty of Prairie du Chien of 1831 set aside 320,819 acres of land near present-day Wabasha as a reserve for the Sioux half-breeds. The half-breeds were expected to settle and take possession of the reserved tract but this did not occur. As the surrounding area was opened for settlement, pressure arose to open the half-breed tract. Half-breed title to the tract was extinguished by dividing the reserve among the enrolled half-breeds and issuing scrip to each individual in proportion to his or her share of the reserve. A total of 640 individuals received scrip to the value of 480 acres, and 38 were issued scrip for 360 acres. The scrip could be used to locate land, surveyed or unsurveyed, anywhere in the public domain. By law the scrip could not be alienated, but this restriction was often evaded and much of the scrip was entered by someone other than the person to whom it was issued.

The abstract for each scrip entry includes the following information: entry or certificate number, number and letter of the scrip, date the scrip was issued, person to whom it was issued, person by whom the scrip was located, date located, legal description of the tract located, date a patent was issued, and volume and page in which the patent is recorded in GLO records. Some entries contain annotations on cancelations, relinquishments, and conflicting claims with citations to letters from the commissioner of the General Land Office.

Arrangement: Chronological by date of entry.

Crookston Land District, 1879-1902. 3 leaves.
Duluth Land District, 1858-1873. 1 folder.
Minneapolis Land District, 1857. 1 folder.
Red Wing Land District, 1857-1861. 1 vol.
St. Cloud Land District, 1859-1860. 1 vol.
Winona Land District, 1857-1868. 1 vol.

Register of Supreme Court Scrip Entries

An abstract of land entries made with "Supreme Court scrip" under provision of acts of Congress of June 22, 1860, March 2, 1867, and June 10, 1872.

The act of June 22, 1860, was intended to settle the remaining claims of individuals or corporations that had received land grants from foreign powers prior to 1846 but whose title to the land had become clouded or lost. The act allowed the United States Supreme Court to decide these cases and to issue scrip as compensation to those claimants who established the validity of their grants. This scrip, commonly known as "Supreme Court scrip," was transferable and most was entered by someone other than the person to whom it was issued. The acts of March 2, 1867, and June 10, 1872, extended the time in which these claims could be brought before the Supreme Court.

The abstract for each entry includes the following information: land office entry number, scrip number, acre/value of the scrip, date of Supreme Court decree awarding the scrip, person to whom the scrip was issued, date the scrip was located (certificate issued), legal description of the tract located, person who located the scrip, and occasional remarks with citations to letters from the commissioner of the General Land Office.

Arrangement: By chronologically assigned entry number.

Crookston Land District, 1879-1894. 17 leaves.
Duluth Land District, July 1874-June 1902. 1 vol. and 1 folder.
Root River Land District, 1879-1880. 1 vol.
St. Cloud Land District, Aug. 1874-June 1885 partial vol.
Winona Land District, 1859-1880. 1 folder.

Register of Surveyor General Scrip Entries

An abstract of land entries made with surveyor general scrip under provisions of an act of Congress of June 2, 1858.

This act was intended to settle outstanding claims of individuals or corporations (mainly in Louisiana, Florida, and Missouri) that had received land grants from foreign powers but had lost the land to settlers or whose title to the land had become clouded. The surveyor general of the district in which the claim was located certified the amount of land lost to the claimant and issued scrip of equal value which could be used to locate land in the public domain. This scrip, commonly known as "Surveyor General Scrip," was transferable and most was located by someone other than the person to whom it was issued.

The abstract for each entry includes the following information: entry number, scrip number, date the scrip was issued, acre/value of the scrip, person to whom the scrip was issued, legal description of the tract located with the scrip, date of location, person who located the scrip, and occasional remarks with citations to letters from the commissioner of the General Land Office.

Arrangement: By chronologically assigned entry number.

Cass Lake Land District, 1904-1905. 1 folder.
Crookston Land District, 1896-1902. 6 leaves.
Duluth Land District, 1872-1873, 1892-1906. 1 folder and 1 vol.
St. Cloud Land District, 1873-1906. 2 partial vols.

Register of Timber Culture Entries

Abstracts of land entries made under provisions of the Timber Culture Act of March 3, 1873.

The abstract for each timber culture entry includes the following information: application or entry number, date of application, legal description of the tract entered, acreage, name of the applicant and county of residence, and fees and commissions paid. Some entries include information on the date of final proof and the eventual disposition of the entry, with citations to letters from the commissioner of the General Land Office.

Arrangement: Chronological by date of application.

Related Records: **Register of Final Timber Culture Certificates** (pages 105-106).

Alexandria Land District, 1873-Feb. 1889. Partial vol.
Crookston Land District, 1873-1891. 0.8 c.f. (4 vols.)
Red Wing Land District, 1873-1885. 1 vol.
Root River Land District, 1883-Feb. 1889. 1 vol.
St. Cloud Land District, March 1889-1895. Partial vol.
Winona Land District, 1886-1897. 1 vol.

Register of Valentine Scrip Entries

An abstract of land entries made in the Duluth land district with Valentine scrip.

Valentine scrip was one of several types of scrip that could be used to enter unsurveyed land. These entries are all for land in township 57, range 17, located in or around Cedar Island or Ely Lake in St. Louis County. Much information regarding the land embraced in these entries can be found in the records of the U.S. Surveyor General (pages 50-57); see especially **Petitions for Surveys**, September 15, 1904.

The abstract for each Valentine scrip entry includes the following information: entry number, scrip number, by whom located, metes and bounds description of the tract located, plat drawings of the tract, various affidavits, and occasional remarks with citations to letters from the commissioner of the General Land Office.

Duluth Land District, 1892-1905. 1 vol.

Rejected Applications to Enter Land

Applications to make homestead and timber culture entries that were rejected or suspended by the register and receiver or the commissioner of the General Land Office. Also included are several applications for leave of absence from homesteads and a rejected townsite entry (no. 2025) for the town of Spooner.

Most of the rejected entries were denied for technical and procedural reasons or because the intended entry conflicted with a previous entry on the tract. The records usually consist of a notice of rejection stating the grounds on which the application was rejected and copies of the homestead application and affidavit. Some include proofs of citizenship and other documentation. The majority of the rejected applications were apparently denied at the time the application was tendered, before an entry number was assigned. A few applications were accepted and then rejected at a later date. These are recorded in the **Register of Homestead Entries** (pages 106-107). Applications suspended by the register and receiver were usually forwarded to the commissioner of the General Land Office for final decision.

Related Records: **Record of Rejected and Suspended Applications and Proofs** (page 100).

Crookston Land District, 1897-1908. 1.5 c.f. (1 box and partial box)

Rejected Homestead Proofs

Homestead final proofs, offered as evidence of compliance with the Homestead Act, that were rejected by the register and receiver or the commissioner of the General Land Office. The series also includes several rejected timber culture proofs.

Most of the rejected or suspended proofs were denied because the applicant failed to meet the Homestead Act's requirements for residence and improvements or because the entry was contested by another claimant. Some were rejected or suspended for technical and procedural errors in filing the proof.

Each rejected proof normally consists of a rejection notice stating the grounds for rejection; affidavits of the claimant giving description of the tract homesteaded, date of settlement, and extent of improvements; and affidavits of witnesses giving detailed information on the claimant's residence on the homestead, extent of cultivation, and a description of the buildings erected and other improvements made. Many rejected proofs are accompanied by other documentation such as proofs of citizenship, reports of GLO special investigators, or correspondence in support of the claimant's proof.

Related Records: **Record of Rejected and Suspended Applications and Proofs** (page 100).

Crookston Land District, 1897-1908. 1.3 c.f. (1 box and partial box)

Serial Registers

Abstracts of land entries made in the three land districts that were still in operation after July 1, 1908. The Serial Register is a consolidated record of all types of land entries and supercedes the various registers for different types of entries.

The abstract for each entry includes the following information: serial number, type of entry (homestead, purchase, etc.), name and address of entryman, legal description of the tract entered, date of entry, and notations of all transactions involving the entry up to the issuance of a patent or cancelation of the entry.

Arrangement: By serial number.

Cass Lake Land District, 1908-1925. 2.0 c.f. (7 vols.)
Crookston Land District, 1908-1925. 4.0 c.f. (13 vols.)
Duluth Land District, 1908-1925. 4.25 c.f. (15 vols. and 4 folders)

NORTHERN PACIFIC RAILWAY COMPANY
LAND DEPARTMENT

Records Regarding Minnesota Lands

The Northern Pacific Railway Company (NP) was chartered by the U.S. Congress (as Railroad Company) in 1864 (13 Stat. 365) and empowered to construct a railroad and telegraph line from Lake Superior to Puget Sound. In return for building the road, the company was granted title to all the odd-numbered sections of land lying within 20 miles either side of the line where it was located in states, and within 40 miles in the territories. This land grant, initially estimated to encompass between 47 and 60 million acres, was the largest ever awarded by Congress. Granted lands in Minnesota totaled over 1.9 million acres.

Because the NP had received its land grant directly from Congress, the lands were transferred to the company from the federal government without the state of Minnesota serving as intermediary. Consequently, the only comprehensive record of NP lands maintained by the state of Minnesota is found in the State Land Office series **Approved Lists: Congressional Railroad Land Grants** (page 10). However, the Division of Archives and Manuscripts also houses the archives of the NP itself. Records of the NP Land Department include several series relating to the selection and transfer of the railroad's grant lands, as well as to the company's subsequent disposition of these lands. Quantities given in the series descriptions below are for the Minnesota portions of those series, unless otherwise noted.

Selection Lists, 1872-1950. 14.0 c.f.
Selections of public lands in Minnesota made by the NP as inuring to it under grants of July 2, 1864, and May 31, 1870. Arranged by U.S. land office: Cass Lake, Crookston, Duluth, Fergus Falls, St. Cloud, and Taylors Falls. Includes selection summaries (1.0 c.f.). A few additional selection records have not yet (1985) been processed.

Patents, 1869-1954. 10.0 c.f.
Each patent is a bound volume conveying certain lands to the railroad from the United States under the NP land grant acts of July 2, 1864, and July 1, 1898. Patents for Minnesota lands include those for the NP (152 vols.), Taylors Falls and Lake Superior Railroad (5 vols.), Stillwater and St. Paul Railroad (1 vol.), and congressional deeds and swamp land deeds to the Lake Superior and Mississippi Railroad and the St. Paul and Duluth Railroad (34 vols.).

Land Cases: Contest Cards, undated. 18.0 c.f.
Cards (8-½ x 14 in.) providing data on the claims of any parties that contested the NP's claim to parcels of land; one card per parcel, arranged by range, township, and section. The cards give the original survey date, names of contestants, type of contest, contest file number, settlement date, contestants' filing and patent dates, and related data.

Land Grant Relinquishments, 1899-1931. 7 vols.

This series of volumes contains the NP's record of granted lands to which it subsequently relinquished ownership. The federal government passed a number of laws from the 1870s to the 1920s (the law most widely cited in these records was passed on July 1, 1898) providing for the disposition of lands that had already been occupied by settlers at the time they were granted to the NP. If the federal government had already sold the land, or if it had been settled in "good faith," the NP was to relinquish ownership and select other land of equal area (indemnity land) in exchange.

The various acts required the secretary of the interior to notify the NP periodically of which lands were to be relinquished. These volumes contain the notices, arranged generally by date, as well as notarized statements by NP officials acknowledging that the lands had in fact been relinquished. The notices list the lands by location (range, township, section, tract) and by claimant (name, homestead application number, and length of residence on the land). Additional relinquishment files have not yet (1985) been processed.

Relinquishments: Letterpress Copies, 1899-1923. 8 vols.

Tissue copies of lists (legal descriptions and acreage) of lands that the NP surrendered to the federal government in exchange for the right to select replacements from indemnity lands. They also include affidavits describing lands already sold by the railroad and therefore exempted from relinquishment. The volumes cover all states in which the NP held granted lands; an index in each volume lists the page numbers for Minnesota lands.

Land Department Miscellaneous Records, 1886-1939. 3 vols.

Certified copies of orders of withdrawal sent to the U.S. General Land Office, 1887-1892 (partial vol.); certified copies of letters filing maps of the general route and definite location, covering all states, 1887 (1 vol.); acceptance by the U.S. president of constructed portions of roads, covering all states, 1886-1891 (1 vol.). Additional miscellaneous land and resources files have not yet (1985) been processed.

Other NP Records

In addition to the specific series described above, correspondence, plats, and other miscellaneous records of the Land Department include considerable information on the process of acquiring, promoting, and selling the land grant; correspondence and minutes for 1870-1876 are available on microfilm and are described in a separate published guide. Numerous series of land and town lot contracts and land sale, lease, deed, and contest records document the subsequent disposition of the granted lands. General land examination records for Minnesota are missing, although there are timber examination reports for 1885-1917. Correspondence and subject files of the president's and secretary's offices, which begin in 1871, contain periodic references to land grant matters. Court case files of the Law Department appear to include many cases relating to ownership and transfer of the grant lands. The records of a few branch lines also include land ownership and sale data, especially those that had received land grants in their own right: Lake Superior and Mississippi Railroad, Little Falls and Dakota

Railroad, St. Paul and Northern Pacific Railway, Stillwater and St. Paul Railroad, Taylors Falls and Lake Superior Railroad, and Western Railroad Company of Minnesota.

LAWS RELATING TO MINNESOTA LANDS

The following is a list of major federal and state laws pertaining to grants of trust fund lands to the state of Minnesota, as they pertain to the records described in this guide. Federal statutes are cited as, for example, 5 Stat. 453; other citations are to Minnesota laws and statutes. More extensive lists and synopses of legislation relating to public and state lands, trust funds, land-related taxation, and railroad grants are found in several of the publications cited in the Bibliography (page 121). Citations to federal laws are taken from Samuel T. Dana, Minnesota Lands.

1841, Sept. 4. Act of Congress (5 Stat. 453).
Granted 500,000 acres to each new state, to be sold for not less than \$1.25 per acre, with proceeds applied to internal improvements (roads, railways, bridges, water courses, and swamp drainage). Also made the preemption privilege general by authorizing settlements on not more than 160 acres of surveyed but unreserved land.

1849, March 3. Organic Act (9 Stat. 403).
Established Minnesota Territory. Reserved sections 16 and 36 in each township for support of schools.

1851, Feb. 19. Act of Congress (9 Stat. 568).
Granted Minnesota two townships (ca. 44,000 acres) for support of a territorial university.

1857, Feb. 26. Statehood (Enabling) Act (11 Stat. 166).
Granted sections 16 and 36 in each township for the support of schools.
Granted 72 sections (46,080 acres) for support of a state university.
Granted 10 sections (6,400 acres) to complete or erect public buildings at the seat of government.
Granted all salt springs in the state, not exceeding 12 in number, each with 6 sections of land adjoining, to be used as the legislature directed.

1860, March 12. Act of Congress (12 Stat. 3).
Extended provisions of the federal swamp land acts of 1849 and Sept. 28, 1850, to the states of Minnesota and Oregon, granting them "the whole of these swamp and overflow lands made unfit for cultivation . . . subject to the disposal of the legislature thereof" (1850).

1861, March 9. Laws 1861, chapter 14.
Provided in detail for appraisal, sale, and leasing of school lands and investment of the income. Created a State Board of Commissioners of School Lands, consisting of the governor, the attorney general, and the superintendent of public instruction, to oversee and keep records of this process. Designated the state auditor as recorder and the state treasurer as receiver.

1861, March 11. Laws 1861, chapter 13.
Created a State Board of Commissioners of Public Lands, consisting of the governor, the attorney general, and the superintendent of public instruction, to begin the survey and selection of state swamp lands and to oversee the survey and management of state lands in general.

1862, March 10. Laws 1862, chapter 62.
Superseded the 1861 laws, establishing a State Land Office to have general supervision of all lands belonging to the state, making the state auditor its ex officio commissioner, and providing in detail for appraisal and sale of school and other lands. Adopted the U.S. Surveyor General surveys as the basis for accepting swamp land designations.

1862, July 2. Morrill Act (12 Stat. 503).
Granted each state 30,000 acres of land for each of its U.S. senators and representatives to support an agricultural and mechanic arts college; entitled Minnesota to 120,000 acres.

1863, March 5. Laws 1863, chapter 12.
Revised the 1862 state law, in particular authorizing the land commissioner to sell pine timber on state school lands.

1865, Feb. 13. Laws 1865, chapter 5.
Appropriated 525,000 acres of state swamp lands for the benefit of an insane asylum, deaf and dumb institute, state prison, and three normal schools, to be selected after title became vested in the state.

1868, Feb. 18 and March 5. Laws 1868, chapters 1 and 55.
Established an agricultural college within the University of Minnesota; provided for the sale of university and agricultural college lands and crediting of the proceeds to a merged permanent university fund.

1870, July 8. Act of Congress (16 Stat. 196).
Allowed a claim by the state of Minnesota to its 1857 grant of state university lands, above and beyond those granted in 1851 to Minnesota Territory.

1870. Laws 1870, chapter 50.
Provided for issuance of a special certificate, in lieu of the original certificate of purchase, to the buyer of tax-forfeited land that had originally been sold as school land.

1872, Nov. 5. Minnesota constitutional amendment (art. 4, sec. 32).
Provided for the appraisal and sale of internal improvement lands granted under the 1841 law, with the proceeds to constitute an internal improvement land fund, not to be appropriated for any purpose without the approval of the electorate.

1873, March 10. Laws 1873, chapter 133.
Transferred salt spring lands to the custody and control of the University of Minnesota board of regents.

1881, Nov. 8. Minnesota constitutional amendment (art. 8, sec. 2).
Provided for the appraisal and sale of all swamp lands and the establishment of a permanent fund, half of the income going to the common school fund and half to support state educational and charitable institutions. In effect, repealed the 1865 law relating to state institutions.

1881, March 2 and Nov. 19. Laws 1881, chapter 104; and Ex. Sess. Laws, chapter 71.
Applied proceeds from sale of internal improvement land to liquidation of Minnesota State Railroad Adjustment Bonds.

1885, March 7 and 9. Laws 1885, chapters 102 and 269.
Prohibited further sale of timber on state lands unless in danger of loss or damage; provided for sale of pine lands after the timber had been sold and removed.

1889, Feb. 28. Laws 1889, chapter 258.
State reform school site in Ramsey County to be surveyed, platted, appraised, and sold, with proceeds credited to the reform school fund. Became D. W. Ingersoll's Addition to St. Paul.

1889, April 24. Laws 1889, chapter 22.
Provided for the sale and lease of state mineral lands, and authorized the land commissioner to reserve to the state all mineral rights when state-owned lands in Cook, Lake, and St. Louis counties were sold.

1891, April 20. Laws 1891, chapter 31.
Transferred internal improvement lands to school lands and university lands, to be sold on the same terms and conditions as school lands, and with the proceeds accruing to the school and university funds.

1895, April 22. Laws 1895, chapter 163.
Altered and specified in great detail many procedures for appraising and selling state lands and timber and for defining and penalizing trespass. Extensively amended in 1905 (Laws 1905, chapter 204).

1899, April 13. Laws 1899, chapter 214.
Designated as forest reserves all tracts set apart from state lands by the legislature or granted to the state by a private party or the U.S. government for forestry purposes, and provided for their management.

1901, April 2. Laws 1901, chapter 104.
Extended the mineral reservation law of 1889 to all state lands except those granted to aid in railroad construction.

1901, April 9. Laws 1901, chapter 177.
Directed the sale of public building lands (all located in Kandiyohi County) and utilization of the proceeds to complete construction of buildings at the state capital.

1907, April 24. Laws 1907, chapter 385.
Transferred state institution lands (selected after the passage of the 1881 constitutional amendment) to swamp lands and the proceeds from their sale to the swamp land fund, half to be credited to the common school fund and half to support state institutions.

BIBLIOGRAPHY

Anderson, Waldemar R., et al. Minnesota Land Ownership: A Study of Land Ownership in Minnesota. St. Paul: Minnesota Outdoor Recreation Resources Commission, 1965. MORRC Staff Report No. [3].

Chase, Ray P. Laws of Minnesota Relating to State Mineral Lands. St. Paul: Minnesota State Auditor, 1930.

Dana, Samuel Trask; Allison, John H.; and Cunningham, Russell N. Minnesota Lands: Ownership, Use and Management of Forest and Related Lands. Washington, D.C.: American Forestry Association, 1960. Includes lists and synopses of land ownership and tax legislation.

Edgerton, A. J. Compilation of the Railroad Laws of Minnesota. St. Paul: William S. Combs, 1872.

Gates, Paul Wallace. History of Public Land Law Development. Washington, D.C.: Public Land Law Review Commission, 1968. Includes an extensive bibliography of additional sources.

Hibbard, Benjamin H. History of the Public Land Policies. New York: Macmillan, 1924.

Iverson, Samuel G. "The Public Lands and School Fund of Minnesota." Minnesota Historical Society Collections 15(1909-1914):287-314.

Johnson, Hildegard Binder. Order Upon the Land: The U.S. Rectangular Land Survey and the Upper Mississippi Country. New York: Oxford University Press, 1976.

Minnesota. Committee on Land Utilization. Final Report: Land Utilization in Minnesota: A State Program for the Cut-Over Lands. Minneapolis: University of Minnesota Press, 1934. Includes historical data.

Minnesota. State Planning Agency. Catalog of Data Sources: Land Use in Minnesota. St. Paul, 1981. Periodically updated.

Orfield, Mathias Nordberg. Federal Land Grants to the States with Special Reference to Minnesota. Minneapolis: University of Minnesota, 1915. Studies in the Social Sciences, No. 2.

Rohrbough, Malcolm. The Land Office Business: The Settlement and Administration of American Public Lands, 1789-1837. New York: Oxford University Press, 1968.

Saby, Rasmus S. "Railroad Legislation in Minnesota, 1849 to 1875." Minnesota Historical Society Collections 15(1909-1914):1-188.